Melanie Klein and Object Relations

An International Journal Devoted to the Understanding of Object Relations

VOLUME 14, NUMBER 2, December 1996

esf PUBLISHERS

BINGHAMTON & CLUJ

INSTRUCTIONS TO AUTHORS

MANUSCRIPTS should be sent to: Prof. O. Weininger, PhD, Editor, Department of Applied Psychology, The Ontario Institute for Studies in Education, 252 Bloor Street West, Toronto, Ontario M5S 1V6, Canada.

MANUSCRIPTS should be typewritten double-spaced, including quotations and references, with one-inch margin on all sides. Send a clearly marked, compatible PC diskette of the manuscript accompanied by two printouts on white paper. Provide an abstract of maximum 250 words, and a brief biographical note with the author(s) degree, title, affiliation, and mailing address.

THE EDITORIAL COMMITTEE welcomes manuscripts which contribute to our understanding of object relations. The length of the paper is usually determined by the content. This may include, for example, critical analyses of concepts, literature reviews leading to creative proposals, empirical research, and historical analyses. The manuscripts may be either theoretical or practical and applied. Notes about cases and treatment procedures, ideas concerning theory, and book and film reviews are invited as well. The highest ethical and professional standards must be observed in protecting the confidentiality of patients, families and groups.

TEXT DOCUMENTATION: Titles of books should be in *italics*, while titles of articles and book chapters in double quotation marks: "..." All notes should be endnotes only with clear and consecutive superscript numbering in the text of the paper. Notes and references should conform to the style in this issue of the publication. References in the text should provide the author name, and in parentheses, the year of the publication of the paper or book. *Example*: Klein (1945) wrote.... If the author's name is not included in the sentence of the text, place in parentheses the author's name, followed by a comma and the year of the publication. *Example*: The focus of my contribution is on... the emotional mathematician (Bion, 1965). For two or more publications, use semicolons to separate the names of authors. *Example*: I have later discovered that the term has been used by others (Kant, 1789; Heidegger, 1931; Wittgenstein, 1933-1935). Whenever material is quoted in the text, cite a page reference, in parentheses, at the end of the quotation. *Example*: If it went... could not endure it and must perish. (p. 586)

REFERENCES should be arranged alphabetically by author. References from the same author should be listed in chronological order, beginning with the earliest source. If there are several papers by the same author, type after the first reference a double em line ——. Names of journals should be in *italics* and abbreviated as in the *Index Medicus*, or in this issue of the publication. Names of books should be in *italics*. For S. Freud's works, indicate the volume number and the pages of the paper from the *Standard Edition*. *Example*: Freud, S. (1915). Observations on transference love. *S.E.* 12: 157-172. However, the first reference to a paper or book by S. Freud from the *Standard Edition* should indicate the editor's name and the complete title of the edition. *Example*: Freud, S. (1915). On beginning the treatment. *S.E.* 12:123-144. In: J. Strachey (Ed.), *Standard Edition of the Complete Psychological Works of Sigmund Freud*, 24 volumes. London: Hogarth Press and The Institute of Psycho-Analysis, 1953-1974. Authors using a different edition or their own translations, should indicate so.

ILLUSTRATIONS AND COPYRIGHTS: All illustratios should be sent in black and white, camera-ready format only. If the illustration is not in camera-ready format, the authors will be billed for the costs incurred by the publisher. The authors of papers published in this journal agree to indemnify this journal and its publisher against any expenses, damages or losses resulting from the use by the author of any unauthorized photographs, words, names, sketches, illustrations (but not limited to) protected by copyright or trademark. Authors are solely responsible for the opinions and views expressed in their papers and do not necessarily reflect the viewpoints of the editor, editorial committee or the publisher.

A COMPLIMENTARY COPY of the issue in which the paper appears and a REPRINT ORDER FORM will be sent to the author(s).

EDITORIAL

O. Weininger

I am sure that the readers and subscribers to the *Journal of Melanie Klein and Object Relations* will be as delighted as I am to know that the journal has a publisher.

Beginning with this issue, the journal will be published by *esf* Publishers, an imprint of the S.F.R. Translation and Publication Fund, Inc. Besides having an excellent record as the publisher of many translations of psychoanalytic books and other texts, *esf* Publishers has a genuine desire to promote an understanding of object relations.

This "new look" of the journal is a much needed improvement. As we know, and you, the reader, have often told us, the content has always been excellent, but the "packaging" was never quite good enough. Now the Journal has both the content and the design.

We are excited in regard to the plans for the journal.

Beginning with 1997, the journal will be published four times a year, in March, June, September, and December.

Whenever possible, we plan to have special issues devoted to a certain topic, book or author.

Aside from articles, book and film reviews will be published regularly. Each issue and volume will be indexed, as well. All books and articles received will be listed under "Books Received" and "Articles Noticed".

We also hope to be able to set up an Internet site in order to communicate more timely with you and receive your suggestions and feedback.

We invite colleagues from all over the world to contribute original papers, letters to the Editor, book/film reviews and news pertaining to professional and scientific events related to our field of interest. We are especially looking to receive original papers and reviews from colleagues living and working in geographical areas of the world which have not been covered in the past in this publication. Interested colleagues and publishers could send us books and articles for reviewing and listing.

I am convinced that the journal will now achieve the international standard and status we have sought and fought for so hard for the past fourteen years. This issue contains an index of volumes 1 through 14, testimony to what we have published since 1983. We are very grateful to all our past and present contributors.

There have been many times when we despaired about the "life" of the journal, but we persisted and have survived. Now we find new hope for the journal, and new goals to accomplish. We invite all our contributors, readers and subscribers to let us know how we are doing. Your feedback and constructive suggestions are needed more than ever.

I hope that you will find the *Journal of Melanie Klein and Object Relations* a true international journal devoted to the understanding of object relations, exciting to read and worth subscribing to.

BION'S "TRANSFORMATION IN 'O'," THE "THING-IN-ITSELF," AND THE "REAL": TOWARD THE CONCEPT OF THE "TRANSCENDENT POSITION"

James S. Grotstein

The author postulates the conception of a "transcendent position," one that both supervenes and transcends the functioning of the paranoid-schizoid and depressive positions but also mediates the infinities and chaos of the Real, in the sense of Heidegger and Lacan. The Real is inclusive of the unmentalized categories such as Kant's "thing-in-itself" and Bion's "beta elements" and "inherent preconceptions." It also relates to Bion's numinous category of "transformation in 'O'." The thesis of this contribution is that the concept of a "transcendent position" helps to unify many of the products of Bion's forays into epistemological, mathematical, aesthetic, spiritual, and mystical explorations of the mind and its functioning. The author employs some selected statements from his personal analysis with Bion and uses them for a springboard to explore Bion's conceptions of intuition, knowing, and transforming in "K" and in "O." In deriving his conception of a "transcendent position" he reassesses the existing Kleinian concept of the depressive position and suggests that it actually serves two discrete phases, one that mediates clinical depressive illness (denial of mourning), and another later one that mediates the pain of the mourning that has finally been accepted. In the past these two positions served dialectically to define one another. The author suggests that they not only define one another, but each and both dialectically mediate the hitherto unrecognized anxiety of the Real, that which is beyond the reach of the imaginary, phantasy-ordering aspects of the paranoid-schizoid position (where " -K" occurs) and equally beyond the symbolic categorizations of the depressive position (where "K" occurs). It is only with the achievement of the "transcendent position" that a "transformation in 'O'" takes place.

Introduction

We are currently witnessing a growing awareness by psychoanalysts and others of Bion's singular virtuosity as an intrepid psychoanalytic visionary, one who was able to confront issues that were either on the outer frontiers of our knowledge or of psychoanalytic respectability—or even beyond. As a polymath and autodidact, he made ingenious use of an astonishing fund of mankind's accumulated wisdom—in philosophy in general, philosophy of science, history, archeology, mathematics, physics, astrophysics, aesthetics, poetry, mythology, logic, metaphysics, and theology, amongst others —in laying the foundation for a new metapsychological metatheory for psychoanalysis, one that was sound both in terms of *objective science* [Transformations in L(ove), H(ate), and K(nowledge)], and also in *intuitionistic* or *subjective science* [Transformations in "O"[1] (Ultimate Truth, Absolute Reality)], in which Bion was a significant pathfinder. What he has forged is both an objective and numinous psychoanalytic epistemology that, according to Meltzer (1978, 1980, 1985), Green (1992), Bléandonu (1994), the Symingtons (1996), and I (Grotstein, 1981a, 1984, 1993) surpasses even that of Freud. Whereas that feat took *genius*, it took *courage* for him to investigate such issues as faith,[2] spirituality, religion, mysticism, metaphysics, and fetal mental life.

Bion was extraordinary in his integration of psychoanalytic metapsychology, metaphysics, theology, and ontology. Virgil had God speak to Aeneas thus, "The clouds that blind thy mortal sight I shall remove." Bion, on the other hand, seems to state, "The clarity that blinds thy mortal sight I shall becloud so that you may be able to intuit '*Ultimate Truth*' and become one with 'O'."[3] He radically and profoundly altered our conceptions of *thinking*, not only by distinguishing the mind from the "thoughts-without-a-thinker," the mind's predecessor that inchoately arose in the infant and required a mind to think these virginal, unthought thoughts, but by also revealing to us that these thoughts and the mind that thinks them are unconscious—that thinking itself is essentially unconscious. What we nominally call "thinking" could best be called "after-thinking" and our known "thoughts" are best called "after-thoughts."

Bion had not only revolutionized psychoanalytic metapsychology and brought it back into alignment with metaphysics and ontology (existentialism), he had also perforated the proud mystique of "objectivity" that had been so sacred to logical-positivistic, deterministic science, the "scientific" establishment that had intimidated Freud and his followers for a century. He revealed its own mythology in its absolute dependence on sense data and reversed the perspective on it and found myths, both collective and personal, to be "scientific deductive systems" in their own right (Bion, 1992). He introduced into psychoanalytic thinking the radical realizations ("catastrophic changes") that followed from the deterministic cosmic view of Newton (K) to the innovative cosmic views resulting from Einstein's theory of relativity and Heisenberg's theory of uncertainty ("O"). Further, he was the first to establish the new "mystical science of psychoanalysis," a numinous discipline based on the abandonment of memory, desire, and understanding. Put another way, Bion was preoccupied with the question of how we know what we know. In his epistemological forays he came to realize the obvious: that we *think* we know the object and the "reality" that contextualizes it by the data of the senses responsive to external reality. Bion was able to show us that what we *think* we know is the emanations of the sense organs[4], i.e., we "know" the object by the impressions that our sense organs emanate from the object's impressions on them. Bion then contemplated the concept of "common sense," by which he meant: (a) the "verdict" of the impressions of each of the sense organs; (b) the consensual "verdict" of the sense organs of the Other ("second opinion"); and (c) the "verdict" of *intuition,* the "seventh servant," the sense organ responsive to internal events. With this overarching epistemophilic instrument, Bion had presented the most nearly complete and effective metatheory that had ever been developed in psychoanalysis.

The focus of my contribution is on Bion, the *intuitionistic epistemologist,* the "emotional mathematician" (Bion, 1965), the "*mystical scientist*" (Bion, 1970), the discoverer and explorer of "O." I address the intuitionistic vertex by proffering the concept of the "*Transcendent Position*" as a way of understanding Bion's mystical or numinous conception of "O." In a similar vein, I shall also briefly put forward another but related idea, that of a "*Transcendent Subject of Being*" (or "Psychoanalytic Subject," who spawns or poses the "Psychoanalytic Object" for analysis [Bion, 1962]), which is associated with the "*Numinous Thinker*" who unconsciously generates ("thinks up") the "thoughts-without-a-thinker," who dreams our dreams while we are asleep, who produces our patients' free associations, who receives our interpretations, and who transforms them into "O." It is the numinous homonuculus of "dream work alpha" (Bion, 1992) who constitutes the "Unconscious Impresario."

I owe the origin of the ideas expressed in this contribution in large part to my own psychoanalytic experience with Bion and also to the encouragement afforded by his concept of "imaginative conjecture" (Bion, 1965, 1970). Further, he himself refers to the idea of "transcendent" on at least two occasions, as I shall cite later (Bion, pp. 75-77), but he nevertheless adheres to the conception of the depressive position in terms of the analyst's access to "O." Here I disagree with him, as I shall show.

Prologue

In order to prepare the reader for my discussion of "O" and for my conceptualization of the "transcendent position," I find it necessary to introduce some of my assumptions ("imaginative conjectures"), but, unfortunately because of space limitations, I can only allude to them. I shall develop them at greater depth in future contributions.

(A) The first assumption is that there is a need to reformulate the psychoanalytic conception of the unconscious as a system and of the id as a structure. In a mathematical re-examination of the unconscious Matte-Blanco (1975, 1988) de-emphasizes the importance of its drives and, instead, highlights the notion that it consists of *infinite sets* specifically and, quantitatively, of *infinity* generally (as in the idea of the boundlessness of pre-symbolic anxiety, i.e., infinite dread, etc.) (Rayner and Tuckett, 1988); Rayner, 1995). The concept of infinite sets can be linked with Segal's (1957, 1981) idea of *symbolic equations*, a pseudo-symbolic, over-inclusive phenomenon occurring in psychosis that can, in turn, be linked with Bion's (1962, 1963) concept of *beta elements*—which he also associates with Kant's *things-in-themselves* and ultimately with "O." I, accepting all the aforementioned associative linkages and mindful as well that Bion too associates the capacity for *infinity* with "O" and the unconscious, reaffirm the concept of the infinity and "frightful symmetry" (Blake, in Frye, 1947) of the unconscious and conclude that, mathematically, it occupies the zero dimension (Grotstein, 1978).

Further, I borrow from Lacan (1966) the concept of the *Register of the "Real,"* by which he means the idea of a dimensionless domain of brute "Reality" that is beyond or before the capacity of the Imaginary or Symbolic Registers (consensual reality) to process or to encode. Lacan's *"Real"* is equivalent to Kant's numinous *"thing-in-itself"* and Bion's "O" (Absolute Reality, Ultimate Truth). The Imaginary and Symbolic Registers optimally render these *numina* into experienced *phenomena*. A failure to be able to render them into phenomena confers upon them the quality—and infinite quantity—of *"nameless dread"* (Bion, 1962, 1963). Parenthetically, when Bion (1965, 1970) writes about the unusually "severe and denuded superego" in psychotics, perhaps he may be referring to its being abnormally reconstituted in the wake of projective attacks by the unmodified (unfiltered by the Imaginary and Symbolic Registers) "Real." Thus, the psychotic superego becomes the repository of infinite dread with omnipotent moral authority.

(B) The next assumption is a need to revise the Kleinian conception of the paranoid-schizoid and depressive positions. Once again, I can only allude to some of the problems and to possible solutions because of space limitations. Briefly put, it is my belief that P-S had been overburdened because of being considered to be: (1) the fons et origine of inchoate mental life, and (2) fundamentally pathological. It is my contention that the schizoid mechanisms that govern mental life in P-S (splitting, projective identification, idealization, and magic omnipotent denial) are equatable with Freud's (1900) conception of dream work (displacement and condensation) and constitutes the *mythopoeic function* that comprises Bion's (1962, 1963) *alpha function* or *dream function alpha*. Thus, P-S mediates "O" and all its associative beta elements (things-in-themselves) by transforming them into *mythemes* (unconscious phantasies) in preparation for transformations in K in the depressive position where they become symbols (no longer phantasies or prephantasmal symbolic equations). As an example of this mythic processing function one can see that the very splitting of experiences with objects into "good"- and "bad"-part-objects constitutes an elementary sorting and differentiating process. Thus, P-S is a pre-symbolic mediator of "O" in preparation for a transformation in K in the depressive position.

As I shall argue later, the depressive position has been overinclusive for too many clinical considerations. Described and explored before her conception of P-S, Klein (1935, 1940) originally conceived of it as a developmental position which mediated infantile (clinical) depression, i.e., the internalization of and identification with objects that had putatively been damaged. She, unlike Freud (1917), did not clearly delineate the difference between true *mourning* and *clinical depressive illness* in the depressive position. As a result, the term "depressive" has acquired a hopeful and desired connotation amongst Kleinians, whereas "P-S" has seemingly become demonized by polarized contrast with it. To me, the depressive position is the mediator of transformations from mythic P-S alpha function to K. Bion (1965, 1970, 1992) informs us, however, that transformations in K are arrived at by sense-based observations, which I am associating with the symbolic transformations that inhere to the depressive position and the consensual sense of reality (K) associated with it, not the metaobservational experiences of transformations in "O," which to me belong to the transcendent position alone.

(C) As a consequence of this reasoning, another position is required, I believe, to do justice to the conception of transformations and evolutions in

"O." I therefore propose the *transcendent position* for that intuitive, ultra-sensual function. Although the term was original with me, I came to discover that it occupied a venerated place in the works of many distinguished philosophers and mystics, as I shall show later. Whereas the infant in P-S does not know the object, only the part-object, the toddler, in the depressive position gets to know the whole object and can symbolize herself/himself in their absence. *In the transcendent position the individual must forsake the presence of the object in order to look inward into his/her own subjectivity; i.e., the transcendent position is the quintessence of a subjectivity that transcends (for the moment) object relations.*

(D) As another consequence of the aforementioned reasoning, I postulate that "O" is the generic metaphysical metaphor for the "dark matter" of our inner and outer world and that it includes all the conceptions hitherto ascribed to the "seething cauldron" (Freud, 1923), "nameless dread" (Bion, 1962, 1963), "chaos" (Winnicott, 1988; Grotstein, 1990), "black hole" (Grotstein, 1990), the horror of the drives (Freud, 1915), and Freud's (1920) and Klein's (1933) respective concepts of the operation of the death instinct. "O" also connotes serenity and harmony, i.e., the capacity to tolerate and therefore reapproximate the inchoate state of aesthetic symmetry. "O" is either horrifying and dreadful or serene, in other words, depending on whether the individual who is in contact with it has or has not effectively *transcended the depressive position and the depressive anxieties associated with it and has also transcended mourning object (K) loss. Psychic reality is "O," not the drives or affects that describe or mediate it.* In mental processing we must experience "O" and then be able to reflect upon it in K and then use this K, with the help of the analyst's "O," to return to higher, ever evolving "O" in a spiraling cycle of transformations.

As a consequence of all the above assumptions, I believe that Bion is saying that the primary, the most fundamental of all anxieties is the ontic, "nameless dread," "O," and that the paranoid-schizoid and depressive positions with their respective persecutory and depressive anxieties constitute techniques or strategies of mediating this ontic terror—through our rescuing our personalness from the Void. Put another way, P-S and D constitute the infant's normal "manic defense" against the Void insofar as they provide a canopy of protective myth (phantasmal [P-S] and consensual [D]).

The Nature of "O"

Perhaps the most far-reaching of his ideas is his formulation of the existence of an ineffable, inscrutable, and constantly evolving domain that intimates an aesthetic completeness and coherence. He variously refers to it as Absolute Truth, Ultimate Reality, or "O." When preternaturally personified, we call it "God," but the latter is a poor pseudonym for it. The "Keter-Ayn-Sof" of the Zohar Kabbalah says it best when it is translated as "Nothing" (Scholem, 1969; Bloom, 1983), a designation Bion (1962, 1963, 1965) was to focus upon as the "no-thing."[5] "O" lies beyond the grasp of the external senses and can only be tentatively experienced by an inwardly receptive sense organ, *intuition*, Bion's "seventh servant," which, according to him, is attainable only by the disciplined abandonment of memory, desire, understanding, sense impressions—and perhaps we could also add the abandonment of ego itself, in the Eastern sense. Intuition is observation's reversible perspective, the latter requiring the senses. Ultimate Reality is also associated with Bion's "beta elements," Kant's "things-in-themselves," Lacan's "Register of the Real," primal chaos (today we would say "complexity"), and yet, paradoxically, primal harmony and serenity, depending on the maturity of our capacity to be "at-one" with it. It was known by Milton (1667) as "the deep and formless infinite" and "the Void," and by Blake (1789-1794; Frye, 1947) as "fearful symmetry" and "frightful fiend." In other contributions I have dealt with this area of numinousness as the "background presence of primary identification" (Grotstein, 1978, 1979).

The concept of "O," beginning with "thoughts-without-a-thinker," the "things-in-themselves," "beta elements," "memoirs of the future," and "inherent pre-conceptions" antedated, anticipated, circumscribed, interpenetrated, and transcended both Freud's concept of the unconscious and its constant conjunction with infantile sexuality as well as Klein's concepts of the paranoid-schizoid and depressive positions. Put another way, Bion revamped Freud's concepts of the id, the unconscious, and the "seething cauldron" and replaced them with an epistemic function, which harkens back to Freud's erstwhile portraiture of the unconscious in regard to the construction of dreams and jokes (Freud, 1900, 1905) before, as Lacan (1966) observed, that Freud deprivileged his conception of the unconscious and turned it into a "seething cauldron," one that was more basic and more primitive than the ego. Klein's conception of the unconscious and of its drives was more sophisticated than Freud's insofar as she envisioned the drives as being essentially object-seeking from the beginning. Nevertheless, the psychology she espoused, primitive and sophisticated as it was, was, like Freud's, essentially deterministic. Bion revealed the ineffable matrix, the container beyond the container of our existence, one that was the eternally unsaturated Void, one that undermines every deterministic certainty with a mocking doubt. In short, the persecutory anxiety of the paranoid-schizoid position and the depressive anxieties of the depressive position constitute emotional lenses that diffract the awesomeness of "O." If experienced too early without these diffracting lenses, we may, like Lot's wife, turn into pillars of salt, i.e., become "orphans of the Real," but if we achieve a reconciliation with ourselves and with our ambivalences toward our objects in the depressive position, we just might qualify for the next karmic progression, that into a sense of *serenity* with the Void, "O," whose very cosmic emptiness allows us to realize our own "O"-ness within.

Bion's Epistemological Odyssey into the "Deep and Formless Infinite"

Bion's first phase of investigation was with the psychology of groups. There he was able to formulate ideas that described how groups became united as well as divided in their functioning. He was ultimately able to bring Klein's ideas about the paranoid-schizoid and depressive positions and of their respective correspondence to group functioning in terms of psychotic anxieties. Further, he was able to show how groups often behave like an individual and how the individual can behave like a group (multiple subselves). In his second phase he clinically investigated the origin and nature of the thought disorders in psychotic patients. In 1959, he began to conceive of one of his most important discoveries, that of "container/contained," in which he helped to transform Klein's intrapsychic psychology into an interpersonal or intersubjective one. In that work he also formulated ideas about how normal thinking begins as the projective identification by the infant of its "fear of dying" into the mother, whose reverie helps her to bear, absorb, and "translate" her infant's dire messages into meaning. He had turned a corner and entered the field of epistemology.

In 1962, beginning with his "Theory of Thinking," his work began to develop even further in the direction of epistemology. Starting with Klein's (1928) concept of the epistemophilic instinct and grafting onto it his new theory of L (love), H (hate), and K (knowledge) *relatedness*, he began having "second thoughts" about his earlier formulations about the psychotic's difficulty in thinking (Bion, 1967). What characterizes his new approach was his changing from a strictly Kleinian emphasis on the intrapsychic destruction of the breast to a destructiveness directed interpersonally and intrapsychically against the L, H, and K *relatedness* (links) to the object (de Bianchedi, 1993). In his next series of contributions, he was able to establish an evolving theorem of epistemological "laws" that included: (1) alpha function, (2) alpha elements, (3) beta elements, (4) constant conjunctions, (5) invariants, (6) reversible perspectives, (7) the grid, (8) "common sense," (9) correlation, and (10) the vertices, as well as many other ideas that together innovatively portrayed how the normal and psychotic person thinks and processes the data of emotional experiences as psychological facts ("K"). The concept of the vertices was far reaching insofar as Bion metatheorized there about the necessity for many different points of view so as to establish a consensus for an ultimate portrayal of Truth. These included the psychoanalytic, religious, mathematical, numinous, etc. It is extraordinary to read the lengths to which he went to understand and to dissect the scientific basis of science itself. In *Cogitations* in particular he goes to great lengths and cites an enormous number of scholars to demonstrate science's own limitations and concludes that psychoanalysis is an emotional, numinous, and mathematical science that is worthy of the name. While especially citing the work of the mathematician Poincaré for his concepts that seem to confirm the importance of the "selected fact," he could also have cited the work of Gödel, the mathematician who like Popper, surveyed the outer limits of feasibility or applicability for any mathematical scheme, scientific theory, etc. (Hofstadter, 1979).

With *Transformations* we now begin to see Bion dealing with Truth as "O," a domain extraterritorial to the reality that we all had taken for granted (Bion, 1965). There he also adumbrated the concept of the *mystic*, whom he analogized with the hero and/or messiah, ideas that he was to develop at greater length in his later work (Bion, 1965, 1970). He had seemingly embarked, as did Ulysses in his second voyage, on the most difficult part of his career. James Joyce's Stephen Dedalus states in *Portrait of the Artist as a Young Man*, "I must leave Ireland and forge in the smithy of my soul the uncreated conscience of my race." Likewise, I believe, Bion left behind the saturated pre-conceptions of the psychoanalytic establishment and ventured inward in a soul-searching, mystic journey with what I have come to believe was a mission to transcend the positivistic certainty of its determinism and "messianically" return it to its provenance in numinous parallax and doubt, where the ultimate mystic and relativistic "science of man" truly resides. What emerged became perhaps the state of the art in psychoanalytic metatheory and metapsychology.

All the while he was forging a psychoanalytic metatheory that was primarily an epistemology based on elements, functions, and transformations relating to the mental and emotional processing of Truth, and based ultimately on the fundamental universality of "O," which stood not only for: (1) ineffable and inscrutable Truth and Reality but also for; (2) the number

"O" ("zero") and its psychic equivalent; (3) "no-thing-ness;" (4) the vertex of the Cartesian coordinates of his grid; and (5) the Other, the Subject (in the self and in the other) that transcends being known or grasped—because of its being the "Subject."

"Common sense," as mentioned earlier comprised the congruence of the individual senses and the matching of that congruence with the consensus of others—to arrive at K, which is then abstracted into its basic common denominators—and then reconstructed into new meanings via intuition. He believed that these transformations always take place in regard to "catastrophic changes" and the inexorable occurrence of "emotional turbulence" (Bion, 1970, 1992). Once he had succeeded "transformations in 'L'" (love), "H" (hate), and "K" (knowledge) in their positive and negative forms and had formulated "transformations in 'O'," it became clearer that he had entered into a hallowed metaphysical domain the only passport to which was the abandonment of emotional and sensual L, H, and K and the use instead of *intuition*. Yet Bion (1965, 1970, 1992) strongly suggests that "common sense," the final arbiter of K and ultimately of "O," represents the conflation, not only of the external senses, both of the individual and of the consensual Other, but also the verdict of the inner sense organ, intuition.

"O" overarches Heaven and Hell in its ultra-majestic, paradoxical sweep. I do not mean to suggest that "O" is only splendored or multifarious. It is what it is and is beyond knowing. What I am suggesting, however, is that the experience of "O" may be dreadful, like the sight of Sodom and Gomorra, the Medusa, or Hades—or beatific and serene, depending on the vertex of emotional maturity and preparedness from which one approaches it. As I have suggested in an earlier contribution and shall suggest later in this work, I believe that we are born into "O" (or the Real, in Lacan's [1966] terminology) and are, we hope, rescued under the beneficent canopy of the organizing and mediating "filters" of the paranoid-schizoid and depressive positions (sequentially, alternately, and in parallel), which mediate and give cosmogonic meaning to the randomness that we would otherwise experience (Grotstein, 1995a, 1995b). Randomness (chaos) is, with mother's reverie, transformed into phantasies and then into symbolic meaning in the depressive position. *Thus, "O" is inchoate and occurs before P-S—and awaits our transcendence of the depressive position so that we may be rejoined—for a moment —with it.* The libidinal and death instincts serve to express and to mediate the infant's distress about its experiences of randomness.

There seems to be an inherent circularity in the concept of "O," i.e., it is within us, around us, and beyond us—as in the mathematical model of the Klein bottle; yet we also temporally proceed from it, through it, and toward it. T.S. Eliot's (1943) phrase, "The end is where we start from..." says it well.

"O," as our mystically directed trajectory fulfills Plato's conception, "That which is always becoming"—but never really attained. It is like Marlowe's description of Tamburlaine's Samarkand, "... always on the horizon, ever distant, always receding." This circularity hints at a cosmic continuum—and even at-one-ment—between the personal Unconscious "O" (immanent or incarnate, in the Heideggerian sense) and cosmically transcendent "O." What Bion had introduced us to was a configuration and existence of a cosmic domain that spatially, temporally, philosophically, and existentially existed beyond our sensual capacity to comprehend, although psychotics and mystics have always known of its existence. One could analogize "O" to be like the mysterious "dark matter" that constitutes the invisible matrix of the universe.

A premature confrontation with "O" before we are processed through the P-S and D positions causes us to undergo an "infantile catastrophe" (Bion, 1962), i.e., we fall into the "black hole" where we become "orphans of the Real." The experience of "O" consequently lies on an existential sliding scale; i.e., we must first traverse through P-S and D in order to achieve the transcendent aspects of "O." To Bion, we become "O" in terms of a transubjective mystical realization, one that transcends knowing, a resonance or "communion in "O'." The object slides under the mystic signifier in order to prepare us for a transient glimpse of fleeting, ineffable Truth. This transformation is totally intra-subjectively meditative. *It is contemplation without an object to contemplate.* By virtue of his injunction to abandon the objects of sensation, Bion not only reaffirmed the rationale for sensory deprivation in psychoanalytic technique (so that we may be enabled to look inward), but he also had joined the ancient tradition of the mystics, such as Meister Eckhart (Fox, 1980, 1981), Ibn'Arabi (Sells, 1994), Isaac Luria (Sells, 1994), and others, and the early Christian and Hebrew mystics, particularly the Gnostics (Pagels, 1979), who had discovered that, through the achievement of asceticism and self-abnegation, one could look inward and find the immanent and incarnate God. What Bion had discovered—or really rediscovered and elaborated upon—was the technique of *intuition*, taken in its literal sense: "looking inward" by foreswearing the glimpse of the external object. "'O' is a dark spot that must be illuminated by blindness," he stated (Bion, 1970, p. 88). Citing a letter by Freud to Lou Andreas Salomé (1966), Bion liberally translated it as follows: "The analyst must cast a beam of intense darkness into the interior of the patient's associations so that some object that has hitherto been obscured in the light can now glow in that darkness" (Bion, personal communication). What he also had come upon, however, was the awareness of the transcending and transcendent awesomeness of our inner (?[6]) world—that what we have called the Unconscious, when released from its positivistic strictures, is, as the Gnostics and mystics have long believed, the inner presence of the "Immanent or Incarnate God," one who is in direct connection with the ineffable and inscrutable "Godhead." It is the Subject of subjects; the unconscious is never meant to be—nor can it ever be—the object. In brief, Bion, standing reverently on Freud's and Klein's supporting shoulders, transcended both instinctual drive, ego, and object-relations theory and helped us find our mysterious way to "Intra-Subjectivity" by daring to rejoin us to that branch of epistemology, metaphysics, that has all too long lurked in the forbidden shadow of psychoanalytic respectability. He was able to formulate a *unified field theory* (metatheory) for psychoanalysis for the first time, one in which "O" served as the common denominator and unifying element that allowed for the continuation of the individual's personal unconscious in the cosmic vastness of ultimate "O."

The Truth and "O"

Associated with his concept of transformations in "O," he delved into the importance of *truth*[7] and its opposite, the *lie*,[8] the former of which was as necessary for mental growth as food was for physical growth, and the latter the negative validation of the truth that needs to be disavowed. Bion believed that the truth spoke for itself and therefore required no thinker, whereas the liar did require a thinker.[9] Seemingly contrary to Freud, Bion seems to valorize the pre-conceptions of the unconscious as the yet unconfirmed intimations of truths that need to be realized by contact with their anticipated "memoir"-counterparts from the future, whereas the ego, in seeking to disguise, repress, or alter the unconscious, becomes disingenuous and dissembles the truth. Bion further distinguishes between the unconscious diffraction of truth as compared with the conscious alteration of it, known as the lie. The role of -K (the lie) is due perhaps to the need for a negative faith to replace the one that either never appeared in sufficient force or which defaulted because of the loss of innocence and the original faith that was necessary to join it in covenant. Here I am alluding to all the demoralizations that accrue from the failure for one to develop a background presence of primary identification. A foreclosure on this entity presupposes that the infant had prematurely plummeted into the Real ("O") before being baptized by the blessed protection of the covenant of parental imagination and conception and therefore predisposes the now hapless one, I believe, to a cataclysmic "orphandom of the Real ('O')" where they feel impelled to swear a new allegiance to their dark (and only) savior, -K. Bion

(1977a) describes this phenomenon as the postnatal persistence of fetal existence in which the fetus becomes prematurely aware of pain and then closes off, and thereby forfeits its developmental and maturational future.

In attempting to pursue the Absolute, ineffable, inscrutable Truth, the Absolute Reality of the psychoanalytic object, he postulated the techniques of "common sense," and "sense, myth, and passion" as stereoscopic locators for ultimate correlation with one's emotions. He subsequently invoked a series of interdisciplinary perspectives that might resist the sensuous pull to which verbal language was subject. He conceived thereupon of the *vertices*, or *perspectives* of (1) *mathematics* and *logic* for their abstract clarifications;[10] (2) *science* for its generalizing capacity of its deductive systems; (3) *myths* for their ability, like scientific deductive systems, to detect *constant conjunctions*; (4) *aesthetics* for its ability to represent the whole preformed gestalt, the backdrop and landscape of Absolute Reality, as it were; (5) the *religious* (or spiritual) because it relates to man's need to worship a God Whom he cannot objectify; and (6) the *mystical* for the elegant simplicity with which one can embrace the Ultimate.

Ultimate Reality, that which is beyond our senses, beyond our imagination, and beyond our conception, belongs to the category of a meta-conceptualization that includes Ultimate Unknowable Truth, chaos, the thing-in-itself, and the so-called "beta elements"[11] evolves. It also includes Plato's theory of Eternal Forms and Bion's "thoughts-without-a-thinker," by which he often means "inherent preconceptions" and also "memoirs of the future," those inherent entities that search for confirming realizations in conjured moieties anticipated in their future. "Thoughts-without-a-thinker" derive from "O." They are the "unborns," the "intimations of immortality" that we seemingly experience to be located within our inner cosmos, but they are placeless, unlocatable; they cannot be found because they can never be the object; they can only enhance our subjectivity.

In his conception of "O" and its association with "thoughts-without-a-thinker" waiting for a mind to think them, we are introduced to the possibility of a conception of mental activity which may perhaps transcend what is ordinarily meant by "thinking." In order to achieve this state, we have to be open, either exploratorily curious or passively unsaturated, but in either case open to and ready for the unexpected. Once we encounter it—perhaps it is better to say that once we are encountered by the unexpected "it" and are able to allow it entry by our readiness to tolerate it (because we are able to attenuate our fears of its potential awesomeness and are thus indeminifed from turning into pillars of salt by its confrontation)—we process it, i.e., in effect we unconsciously stamp it with the imprimatur of our personalness (autochthony), that is, we allow ourselves to "create" it imaginatively before "discovering" it and then allow it to be internalized and enter into the digestive alchemy of transformation. It must be noted that "thinking" for Bion is not necessarily a conscious, intentional act. By allowing familiarity with the unfamiliar, we are allowing thoughts-without-a-thinker to be thought about by a receptive mind that realizes the presence of its lost yet nevertheless remembered echo-moiety from its future, which now has a home-mind in which it can play and be played with—thoughtfully—in the preconscious. Thus, August von Kekulé could discover the yet unknown and unsuspected hexagonal ring of carbon molecules that defined the aromatic series of chemicals, but not through conscious thought. He could only intuitively anticipate this thought without a thinker. It was in his dream that the realization was able to make its dramatic and historic epiphany.

The "thinker who thinks the thoughts" is akin to the "dreamer who dreams the dream" and the "dreamer who understands the dream" (Grotstein, 1981b). The "thinker who understands the thoughts" is the constantly expectant internal playmate of this unsaturated, disciplined, unconscious thinker. Together, they patiently await the entry from the future of their long exiled unknown but always suspected "thought without a thinker," who becomes their transient infant thought as it transforms them into a new childless but expectant empty couple of the next epistemic generation. The point is that thoughts seem to think themselves if we are optimally able to allow them their intercourse in our receptive containers. Perhaps what we call thinking, consequently, constitutes the afterthoughts and "bare-bones" derivates from a numinous thinking couple.

To these ideas I would also add yet another relevant idea from the *Kaballah*, the mystic Hebrew text in which Bion was deeply interested (personal communication). In the Kaballah, according to Bloom (1983), there once was a unitary Godhead, but, in order for the world to be created, He had to "shrink" from His Godhead ("Keter-Ayn-Sof" ["Nothing"][12]) in order to become immanent. The immanent God has been referred to in Greek texts as the "Demiurge," the creator of the world. When we are in a state of "transformation in 'O'," we feel at one with the Godhead itself, the Ultimate Subject. God, the Demiurge, is the colloquial way in which we innocently yet sacrilegiously refer to Him as the Object, which He never can become. In that state we once would have "turned into a pillar of salt" because of our terror of experiencing it. Ultimately, if we can face it, we are in that state of *serenity* that is experienced by the mystic. Yet we must also be prepared for the dark face of "O," i.e., "O's" reversible perspective, the ineluctable journey to which Bion (1979) cryptically refers to as "Dawn of Oblivion," which at the same time constitutes Bion's ultimate theory of eschatology.

Alpha Function and "Dream Work Alpha" Container/Contained

The field in which the analyst's intuitionistic technique becomes operant was termed *alpha function* by Bion (1959). Starting with Freud's (1911) concept of two principles of mental functioning (primary and secondary process), Bion seems to have united them as indivisible complementary functions under the rubric of alpha function, which originates in mother's reverie as she absorbs, detoxifies, and then "translates" her infant's cries of distress into acceptable meaning. Eventually the infant introjects mother's alpha function and becomes a "thinker" on its own. In his *Cogitations*, however, Bion (1992) uses the term *"dream work alpha,"* a concept that he never had employed in his hitherto published works, one which suggests a connection to Freud's (1900) concept of unconscious *"dream work."* The penumbra of meanings associated with this latter term convey unusual intimacy on the part of the analyst toward the patient. It suggests that the analyst must "dream" (daydream) the patient, which to me conveys the idea that the analyst must *absorb the essence* of the patient. His concept of alpha function had already long ago altered the definition of projective identification from an intrapsychic to an interpersonal one. It also helped launch a new respect for alleged countertransference phenomena and, even more to the point, significantly anticipated the advent of the *intersubjective* paradigm. On another level, however, I infer that Bion's overall conception of alpha function or dream work alpha is inclusive of: (1) the mythopoeic (phantasy/dream-creating) function of P-S; (2) the symbolizing function of the depressive position; and (3) the "common sense" collation of the individual functions of the observational senses in common, the intersubjective consensus, and the consensus with intuition (obtained through reverie, i.e., meditation).

Of relevance in this contribution is that aspect of dream work alpha that suggests that both parties, the analyst and the patient should "surrender," as it were, to the analytic experience, i.e., that they both enter into a meditative-like trance.[13] In this contribution I shall argue that this "surrender" presupposes that the analyst, whose disciplined behavior allows the patient the experience of reasonable safety in the analytic procedure, has already "transcended" (in the Jungian sense of regular, successive developmental progression) his own persecutory anxieties Klein's (1940) of the paranoid-schizoid position and also the depressive anxieties (manic and depressive defenses against mourning and against acknowledgment of dependency on the object). Bion (1970) is very specific about the requisite experience for the analyst:

In every session the psycho-analyst should be able... to be aware of the aspects the material that, however familiar they seem to be, relate to what is unknown both to him and the analysand. Any attempt to cling to what he knows must be resisted for the sake of achieving a state of mind analogous to the paranoid-schizoid position. For this state I have coined the term "patience" to distinguish it from "paranoid-schizoid position".... I mean this term to retain its association with suffering and tolerance of frustration.

Patience should be retained without "irritable reaching after fact and reason" until a pattern "evolves". This state is analogous to what Melanie Klein called the depressive position. For this state I use the term "security".... I consider that no analyst is entitled to believe that he has done the work required to give an interpretation unless he has passed through both phases—"patience" and "security".... In short, a sense of achievement of a correct interpretation will be commonly found to be followed by a sense of depression. (p. 124)

It is at this very point that I should like, not so much to differ with Bion's technical advice, but to modify and to extend his brilliant and innovative idea. As I shall soon argue, I believe that there are three, not two, positions involved in the analyst's reverie-containment mode (the third being the "transcendent"), and three requisite affects apposite to them: "patience," "security," and "serenity," the last of which I believe even "transcends" the experience of security, the latter of which implies security from depressive anxieties, whereas the former has proceeded beyond that.

The "Transcendent Position"

In a recent contribution I posited, after proffering a reappraisal of Klein's concept of the depressive position, the consideration that Bion's metapsychological and metaphysical efforts seemed to anticipate the concept of a *transcendent position*, one which encompasses "O" by being "O" itself. Unlike the paranoid-schizoid and depressive positions, it is a position to which entry is restricted to the total suspension of object seeking and object awareness (Bion, personal communication, 1972) although the presence of the object, paradoxically, is necessary. Put succinctly, the paranoid-schizoid position is largely associated with the mediation of *L and H linkages* in terms of *phantoms*, i.e., internal objects that are products of unconscious phantasies of part-objects intermixed with part-selves. The depressive position, on the other hand, is associated with *K linkages* in terms of beginning discoveries about the separateness of the whole object. It is the maturation of the K linkage that allows the infant, patient, and analyst to *evolve in "O,"* which I term the achievement of the *transcendent position.*

Background of the Term "Transcendent"

I first came upon the term transcendent when reading Bion's works and only later discovered that it had been used by Kant (1787), Wittgenstein (1933-1935), Heidegger (1931, 1968), and by Jung (1916) and some of his followers (Dehing, 1993; Solomon, 1994). Bion (1970) refers to transcendence as follows:

> My object is to show that certain elements in the development of psycho-analysis are not new or peculiar to analysis, but have in fact a history that suggests that they *transcend*[14] barriers of race, time, and discipline, and are inherent in the relationship between the mystic and the group. (p. 75)

—and on the next page:

> One result of separation [between man and his god] is no direct access of the individual to the god with whom he used formerly to be on familiar terms. But the god has undergone a change as part of the process of discrimination. The god with whom he was familiar was finite; the god from he is now separated is *transcendent*[15] and infinite. (p. 76)

Transcendence carries in its sweep an epistemological tradition that began amongst the pre-Socratic philosophers, flourished in Plato, continued in other forms in the so-called "mysteries," (Orphic, Eleusinian, and others), traversed through the ancient Hebrew and early Christian mystics, became prominent in the Gnostic Gospels and in Zoroastrianism and later with so-called apophatic mystical writers such as Meister Eckhart, Ibn'Arabi, John Scotus Eriugena, Marguerite Porete, Plotinus, surfaced again in the Zohar Kabbalah, became bleached out by the glare of the Enlightenment and further dismissed by the proud certainty and determinism of logical positivism, surfaced briefly with the transcendalistic movement of Carlyle and Emerson in the nineteenth century, and resurfaced in yet another way in the mystical works of Kierkegaard. Elsewhere it arose as a Zoroastrian revival in the works of Nietzsche and played a prominent position in Schreber's *Denkwürdigkeiten.*

The mystic seed took root in metaphysics. It appeared as such in Hegel and especially in Kant's (1787) *Critique of Pure Reason* as the epistemological quest for the transcendent, particularly the "transcendent aesthetic," a concept that was to find its consummate expression in the existential literature, such as Sartre and particularly the works of Heidegger, the latter of whom left us the legacy of his obsession with the nuances implicit in the subjectivity of Being—in contrast to Hegel's legacy of the object. Jung was the first psychoanalyst to appreciate its importance. Mysticism has long been claimed both by religion and by epistemology. Spiritualism overarches both areas. Lacan had the profoundest respect for mysticism, and the totality of his works can be read as an appreciation of its importance in mental life. Bion also had great respect for the presence in man of what he termed the "moral or religious instinct." Not formally religious himself, he was one of the profoundest secular mystics of ours or any time—certainly within psychoanalysis—as well as its foremost epistemologist generally—and this includes Freud. Briefly put, Bion's works represent a consummate distillation of the collective wisdom of Western and Eastern civilization and is focussed on the episteme of how man seeks and hides from the ineffable. Reality, better known in its limited sense by most psychoanalysts as "external reality," had become so saturated that it shrunk into a positivistic enclave.

Heidegger (1931/1962) explores transcendence from a metaphysical and existential vertex. He distinguishes between *theological* and *epistemological transcendence.* I shall now quote from Heidegger (1968) who also refers to Kant's use of transcendence:

> Transcendence, in the Kantian sense, is above all, oriented to two possible ways of grasping the being-in-itself, on two essentially different sorts of intuition.... We must therefore distinguish the thing-in-itself qua appearance and qua thing-in-itself. (1) Proceeding from the correctly understood concept of the thing-in-itself, one can validly deduce the concept of appearance qua "finite" object. (2) Proceeding from appearance, one can show the "X" immanent in it qua thing itself, which is not, however, the "thing-in-itself" in the strict sense. (p. 164)

And on the next page:

> Transcendence is... the primordial constitution of the *subjectivity*[16] of a subject. The subject transcends qua subject; it would not be a subject if it did not transcend. To be subject means to transcend. (p. 165)

And later in the same work:

Transcendence is being-in-the world. Because it pertains to transcendence as such, world is a transcendental concept in the strictest sense of the term. In Kant "transcendental" has a meaning equivalent to ontological but pertaining to the ontology of "nature" in the broadest sense. For us the term has the meaning equivalent to "fundamental ontolological." (p. 170)

Whereas Heidegger's use of the the term transcendence closely approaches that of Bion, particularly Bion, the existentialist and mystic, Jung's (1916) use of transcendence seems more general in its application to development. He defines it thus:

"It means a psychological function" (CW 8, paragraph 131), "combined... of conscious and unconscious elements" (CW 6, par. 184), "a... discursive cooperation of conscious and unconscious factors" (CW 10, par. 855). It is called transcendent "because it makes the transition from one attitude to another organically possible, without loss of the unconscious" (CW 8, par 145) and "because it facilitates the transition from one psychic condition to another by means of the mutual confrontation of opposites" (CW 11, par. 780). The transcendent function "unites the the pairs of opposites" (DAI, p. 648; CW 14, par. 261; CW 18, par. 1554). It is linked closely with symbol formation.... (Dehing, 1993, p. 16)

Ricoeur (1970), in his discussion of hermeneutics, says the following:

The only radical way to justify hermeneutics is to seek in the very nature of reflective thought the principle of a *logic of double meaning*,[17] a logic that is complex but not arbitrary, rigorous in its articulations but irreducible to the linearity of symbolic logic. This logic is no longer a formal logic, but a *transcendental*[18] logic established on the level of the conditions of possibility...Thus the logic of double meanings, which is proper to hermeneutics, is of a *transcendental*[19] order. (p. 48)

The "Transcendent Position" as the Position of "Serenity"

The "transcendent position" represents the achievement of the state of meditative-like grace in which one experiences a serenity that transcends conflict. One is now beyond the ontological skirmishes of the paranoid-schizoid position and the lugubrious agonies of the depressive position. One has achieved the capacity for mourning, reparation, empathy, tolerance of ambivalence, and true love and caring. One must then continue his/her ontological pilgrimage to the next state, one of enlightenment and serenity where one is at peace with oneself and with the world, both internal and external. Whereas, when one was unprepared as an infant to confront the denizens which occupied the Register of the Real (e.g., chaos, beta elements, the things-in-themselves, inherent preconceptions, the "shadow side of God," the noumenon), one now as an individual who has "learned from experience" is privileged to be able to achieve serenity and to be at peace within the entire range of the Register of the Real. In its comprehensive capacity for "at-one-ment" the transcendent position reconciles virtually all the "vertices" or cosmic perspectives which inform Bion's higher epistemological endeavors, i.e., the scientific, mathematical, spiritual, mystical, noumenal, and aesthetic, to which I now add the transcendent.

> For we know in part, and we prophesy in part.
> But when that which is perfect is come, then that which is in part shall be done away.
> When I was a child, I spoke as a child, I understood as a child, I thought as a child; but when I became a man, I put away childish things.
> For now we see through a glass darkly; but then face to face; now I know in part; but then shall I know even as I am known.
> And now abideth faith, hope, charity, these three; but the greatest of these is charity.
>   (Paul's First Letter to the Corinthians, 13: 9-13)

The Concept of "O" as a Revision of the Nature of the Unconscious

Bion (1965, 1970) frequently cites Milton's phrase, "the deep and formless infinte" when he writes about "O." In so doing, he, and Matte-Blanco (1975, 1988) as well, ascribe the quality of infinity (dimensionally), of infinte sets (mathematically), and of chaos or complexity cosmically to the Unconscious. Freud's and Klein's perspectives on the nature of the unconthoughts without-a-thinkerscious were fundamentally constrained by their their positivistic and deterministic assumptions. The most elemental component of the infant's mental mental life, the "forme fruste" or "first cause," as it were, was considered to be the libidinal and destructive drives. Begining with Winnicott's (1954/1988) concept of "chaos" and Bion's (1965) concept of "O," as well as Matte-Blanco's (1975, 1988) concept of infinite sets, we begin to see a postmodern revision of the picture of the fundamental nature of the Unconscious. The "deep and formless infinite" is its nature. It is dimensionless, infinite, and chaotic. In other words, Bion's picture of the

Unconscious, along with that of Winnicott and Matte-Blanco, conveys an ineffable, inscrutable, and utterly indefinable inchoate formlessness that is both infinite and chaotic—or complex—by nature. It is what it is and is always changing while paradoxically remaining the same. From this point of view, the instinctual drives of Freud and the paranoid-schizoid and depressive positions of Klein can be understood as secondary structures, strategies or filters, as it were, to help the infant, child, and adult mediate this chaos. Lacan (1966), in delineating this aspect of the Unconscious as the "Register of the Real," as distinguished from the "Registers of the Imaginary and the Symbolic," fortifies my view of Bion's conception of the Unconscious as inchoately chaotic—vis-à-vis any attempt to "understand" it or perceive it. The Unconscious, as the Subject of subjects, is "O" and is therefore, like the "Godhead" with which it is associated, utterly uncontemplatable. The only way to access it is by resonance in "O" with it.

Chaos and infinity belong to, to borrow a term from Derrida, the "always already" formed transcendent position of the numinous thing-in-itself awaiting the act of creation. P-S organizes and mediates the horror of its awsome chaotic infinity by transforming beta elements into phantasies. In the depressive position the phantasied part-objects are transformed into symbolic whole objects (K), which undergo the depressive and manic defenses against depressive anxiety and then undergo mourning. The successful mourner is then enabled to undergo a shift to a loftier but fleeting state, the transcendent, where serenity, composure, equanimity, and harmony are possible for brief moments. One is not able to transcend in it until one has been able to tolerate, first the persecutory anxieties of the P-S and then the depressive anxieties, ambivalences, and mourning that inhere in the depressive position. Once there, one can be in communion with a sense of an Absolute Truth that one can tolerate never really knowing, i.e., Truth lies in the gap made possible by parallax.

What I believe that Bion had ultimately learned from his study of psychotics—and from liars too, for that matter—was that the psychotic, like the liar, is, by default, closer to "O" than to "K." In other words, the psychotic is not able sufficiently to exercise his "privileges" in the Registers of the Imaginary (unconscious phantasy) or the Symbolic. A precocious exposure to "O" is therefore his/her curse and default position. The psychotic, like the liar, confuses "O" with "K," whereas the normal and the neurotic individual confuse "K" with "O." By this I mean that psychotics confuse our sense of external reality with the thing-in-itself—without imaginary or symbolic disguise, whereas the normal or neurotic individual, being protectively screened from the "thing-in-itself"—may not even know that it exists, were it not for the mystics such as Bion. They are talking about different realities.

The Dialectic Between P-S and D and (P-S and D) and the Transcendent Position

Earlier, we conceived of there being a horizontal dialectical tension between the split egos and internal objects within the paranoid-schizoid position (P-S [BO][20]↔P-S[GO][21]). Bion added the concept of the reversible dialectical tension between the paranoid-schizoid and depressive positions (P-S↔D). With his conceptions of "nameless dread," the "thing-in-itself," and "O" he strongly hints, I believe, that there exists yet another dialectical tension, one between each of the two known positions and "O," the transcendent position (P-S↔D)↔"O."

"The Transcendent Subject of Being"

Perhaps the quintessence of my theme about the transcendent position is the concept of the presence of a *"Transcendent Subject of Being,"* which the analyst and his patient become or approximate becoming when a transformative evolution in "O" occurs, i.e., a resonance with one's own respective "O" as well as the "O" that is communal between them. The experience constitutes an epiphany in which one, for that exquisite moment, becomes the *"Numinous Thinker"* of *"the thoughts-without-a-thinker,"* which in psychoanalysis would correspond as the *Subject* to Bion's (1962, 1963, 1965, 1970) consideration of the *"psychoanalytic object."* In an earlier contribution in tribute to Bion, I proffered the concept of the *"Dreamer Who Dreams the Dream"* and the *"Dreamer Who Understands the Dream"* as a composite unconscious Subject who initiates the production of dreams, analytic free associations, etc. and who understands them (Grotstein, 1978, 1981b, 1984). Today, because of my careful rereading of Bion on the subject of "understanding," I should modify the latter concept to that of the *"Dreamer Who Resonates with the Dream."* I am postulating, in other words, that there exists a *Coherent Presence,* an *Intelligence,* or *Wisdom*[22] that is preternatural in nature, that can be understood to function as a putatively "divine" creator and organizer of unconscious mental life, including our (?) spontaneous free associative "thoughts-without-a-thinker" and arranges rendezvous for them with the "selected fact" that, in turn, arranges for further rendezvous with the objects that await their rendezvous with the "memoirs of the future." Put another way, the concept of the "transcendent subject of being" can be associated with the teleological perspective. Samuels, Shorter and Plaut (1989) cite Jung's (1954) teleological perspective as follows, "It is not I who create myself, rather I happen to myself" (p. 291). The self, according to this teleological perspective, has an a priori existence and is the hidden operator behind our lives. This concept helps us to conceive of the possibility of an ultimate rendezvous with our numinous, teleogical archetype ("Now through a glass darkly, then face to face...").

The Evolution from Object Relations to Subjectivity

As I have already suggested, Bion, like Lacan, moved away from his background in object-relations toward the phenomenon of the Subjectivity of Being and found, as did the mystics, that Being experiences its own Beingness transcendently if it is in a state of meditation in empty thought-fulness, i.e., without an object to disguise its self-awareness. At the same time, paradoxically, Subjective Being can be revealed to itself only in the presence of an object whose ineffable Otherness is experienced. I proffer the term the "Transcendent Subject of Being" as an ontic (existential) way of designating the Unconscious as an ineffable "I" (Other "I") that is *Other* to the "I" of the speaking self, the ego, which at the same time is its "channel" to the other. Put succinctly, this Numinous Subject is both higher and profounder, and may be what Nietzsche (1883) meant by *das Übermensch*, which I translate as "higher man."

Finally, we come to the "Numinous Thinker," who "thinks" the "thoughts-without-a-thinker." This "Numinous Thinker" dreams and understands our dreams, creates and arranges free associations for analysis, and ultimately puts the analyst's interpretations to use by allowing their transformation from "K" to "O" where it can enter into the numinous alchemy of internal change. Thus, the "Numinous Thinker" can be thought of as the "homunculus of dream work alpha" and is the mystical agent who mediates the miracles of transformation. In his forge "K" is transformed into "O" and enters into growth. Then a new cycle takes place in which the patient's "O" becomes transformed by his Numinous Analytic Subject into revelations in K to the analyst about his (the patient's) "Analytic Object." The analyst, in turn, is enabled to discern the "Analytic Object" with the assistance of the "selected fact" (that gives the hitherto chaotic data a sense of coherence). The analyst's "O" is thereby able to transform the "K" of the patient's "Analytic Object" ("O") into his own "O" and share this "O" interpretively with his patient in a state of transcendent reverie once more. In other words, a continuous cycle of transformations occurs.

What Bion had apparently tapped into was a universal cycle of "mental digestion" in terms of Truth that corresponds unusually closely to the Krebs Cycle for the intermediate metabolism of carbohydrates in biochemistry. He had come up with a metapsychological metatheory that united many fields of epistemology. My own proposed additions to his metatheory is to append the conception of an additional position and the conception of a mystical "Thinker," a numinous homunculus, who acts as a "divine impresario" for the psyche in its successive cyclic transformations and alchemical metamorphoses.

The "Transcendent Position" as the Position of "Serenity"

The "transcendent position" represents the achievement of the state of meditative-like grace in which one experiences a serenity that transcends conflict. One is now beyond the ontological skirmishes of the paranoid-schizoid position and the lugubrious agonies of the depressive position. One has achieved the capacity for mourning, reparation, empathy, tolerance of ambivalence, and true love and caring. One must then continue his/her ontological pilgrimage to the next state, one of enlightenment and serenity where one is at peace with oneself and with the world, both internal and external. Whereas, when one was unprepared as an infant to confront the denizens which occupied the Register of the Real (e.g., chaos, beta elements, the things-in-themselves, inherent preconceptions, the "shadow side of God," the noumenon), one now as an individual who has "learned from experience" is privileged to be able to achieve serenity and to be at peace within the entire range of the Register of the Real. In its comprehensive capacity for "at-one-ment" the transcendent position reconciles virtually all the "vertices" or cosmic perspectives which inform Bion's higher epistemological endeavors, i.e., the scientific, mathematical, spiritual, mystical, noumenal, and aesthetic, to which I now add the transcendent.

An "Imaginative Conjecture" on Bion's Personal Relationship to "O"

Bion arrived at this new concept of transformation *and* evolution in "O," first by intuiting the existence (presence) of the absent breast, the "nothing," in the clinical situation. He may also have arrived at it from having experienced the terrors and traumas of his own life, according to Meg Harris Williams (1985).[23] When we read in his autobiography that he "... died on the Amiens/Roye Road on August 8, 1917," we get a haunting piece of subjective archive that informs us with graphic certainty that he had been baptised into, and thus had become an "orphan of the Real" and had been certfied in the experience of "nameless dread" (Bion, 1982). Who could be more qualified to be our guide in that indescribable domain, the very existence of which most of us are privileged never even to have suspected. In regard to those experiences, one wonders that in his few but trenchant critiques of Klein, his analyst, in his autobiography if he were not suggesting that Klein effectively analyzed the envy, greed, and omnipotence of the putatively surviving Bion (i.e., she helped him to evolve from P-S to D), but she may have neglected the "dead" one, the one who was amberized on the holocaustal side of "O." Bion, who had been nominated in the field for the Victoria Cross and had received the D.S.O, always maintained that he was a "coward." This paradox is understandable if we think of him as having suffered from what we now prosaically term a "post-traumatic stress disorder," in which he may have believed that he had surrendered to the darkness of dread. His autobiography and metapsychology may constitute desperate "radio signals" from an "undead"/"dead" self who is struggling to be heard—from the other side. When he spoke of "making the best of a bad deal," we perhaps begin to realize that, in his attempted rehabilitation from that ultimate trauma, he was trying to put his agony, surrender, and reconciliation to optimum use—to experience hope under the forboding shadow of intimidating dread and demonstrate to us how to use our sublimated agony as an analytic instrument.

Personal Reminiscences of Bion as Analyst

After reading *Cogitations,* I had gradually begun to realize that these ideas naturally emerged in me, not only from my re-reading of Bion's other works, but also from the spontaneous distillation of the pageant of memory of my analysis with him. Some of the evocative and yet apposite ideas that his interpretations (actually, my transformations of them) include the following: —"The more that one progresses in analysis, the more one realizes the presence of a rapidly burgeoning unknown." "Despite all our attempts to fix names and ideas to your painful feelings, we shall never know their source. It is lost ineffably in mystery. We can only approximate it, and not very satisfactorily at that." On another occasion when I had referred in passing to Melanie Klein, he asked, "Did you know Melanie Klein? How did you know her? Or did you know about her?"

The remainder of the session—and of the analysis—was devoted in no small measure in trying to come to grips with the question of how I came to believe that I knew anyone or anything. On yet another occasion he proffered an interpretation to me that I felt was profound and extraordinarily moving. My response to it was, "That was a beautiful interpretation!" His counter-response was memorable. "Yes, a beautiful interpretation, you say. The snag is (one of his favorite expressions) that my 'beautiful interpreta- tion' was made possible by your 'beautiful associations.' I was only offering you a 'second opinion' (another of his favorite expressions) about them! You were so keen on listening to me that you neglected to listen to yourself speaking to me—and, for that matter, to yourself listening to yourself listening to me!" His follow-up interpretation was not only his attempt to interpret the danger of my idealization of him and his utterances rather than consider them as "food for thought." They harkened to a profounder level of interaction between us to which I had hitherto been unaware. When I read about "dream work alpha" in his *Cogitations*, especially his notion that, just as the mother must "dream" her infant, the analyst must "dream" his/her patient, I had a veritable "déjà vu." I then realized that Bion had been introducing me to the quintessence of the authenticity (truth) of "learning from experience," i.e., *I learn from him only from what I learn from how I initiate my spontaneous utterance to him (the "thought without a thinker") and how I respond to his "second opinion" of it!*

As consequence of those experiences, particularly the last mentioned, I began to appreciate the emphasis that Bion seemed to be placing on "looking inward," i.e., valorizing *intuition*, that sense organ that is sensitive to internal psychic qualities. I also recalled in association with that "inward looking" Bion's love of poetry and in particular his oft-recited lines from Milton's *Paradise Lost:*

> ...Thus with the Year
> Seasons return, but not to me returns
> Day, or the sweet approach of Ev'n or Morn
> Or sights of vernal bloom, or Summer's Rose,
> Or flocks, or herds, or human face divine;
> But cloud instead, and ever-during dark
> Surrounds me, from the cheerful ways of men
> Cut off, and for the Book of knowledge fair
> Presented with a Universal blank
> Of Nature's works to mee expung'd and raz'd,
> And wisdom at one entrance quite shut out.
> So much the rather thou Celestial light
> Shine inward, and the mind through all her powers
> Irradiate, there plant eyes, all mist from thence
> Purge and disperse, that I may see and tell
> Of things invisible to mortal sight.
>
> (Book III, lines 40-55, pp. 100-101)

Yet I cannot conclude without citing another mystic poet:

> What we call the beginning is often the end
> And to make an end is to make a beginning.
> The end is where we start from....
> We shall not cease from exploration
> And the end of all our exploring
> Will be to arrive where we started
> And know the place for the first time.
> Through the unknown, remembered gate
> When the last of earth left to discover
> Is that which was the beginning....
>   (T. S. Eliot, 1943, "Little Gidding" from *Four Quartets*)

Summary

Bion was foremostly an analytic epistemologist whose professional life was dedicated to answer "how we know what we know." In transcending the verdict of the external, observational senses, he was able to show us "O," the dominion of beyond the senses that exists beyond us yet within us—but beyond our reckoning. His concept of "O," "Ultimate Truth," "Absolute Reality," constitutes an important contribution to psychoanalytic metapsychology. With it, we are able to contemplate a domain of our existence that is beyond, i.e, transcends, what we had hitherto been able to conceive. I believe that the concept of the transcendent position allows us to conceptualize the life cycle of the individual and his ability to tolerate and confront the "Real," that domain that exists beyond our "reality." The infant is too frightened and must therefore dilute or evade it with persecutory -K phantasies. Following this he may accept the realities in K of the objectively knowable (symbolic) reality of others. It is only in the transcendent position that he is able to come to peace—and be at-one— with its presence and its ineffability. Then, he, as the mystic or messiah, is in a state of serenity—and can see the stars in daylight! I put it thus: P-S⇌TP; DP⇌TP; (P-S⇌DP)⇌TP. From these perspectives one may hypothesize that Bion, in adding these multiple vertices (dimensions) to psychoanalytic epistemology shifts the emphasis of ultimate terror from the instinctual drives to "the thing-in-itself," i.e., inchoate chaos, the inherent pre-conceptions ("memoirs of the future"),[24] and the absoluteness of the infinity and ineffability that characterize them. We have an ultimate rendezvous to keep with them when we are finally able to achieve confidence in our L, H, and K links (PS⇌D) and can transcend to the transcendent position where we can recognize "O" face-to-face (no longer "through a glass darkly"), and can be in a state of acceptance, serenity, and an at-one-ment with "O."

Presented at the Panel "Bion's Contribution to Psychoanalytic Theory and Techniques" at the 39th International Psychoanalytic Conference in San Francisco, CA on Monday, July 31, 1995.

NOTES

1. I shall employ the quotation marks around "O" in order to designate its ineffability and inscrutability. "O," like "God" or even "I," can never really be the *object*, whether in grammar, discussion, or even in speculation. This is my way of attempting to adhere to the "mystical language of unsaying," according to which principle the ineffable can only be referred to "apophatically," that is, by saying and then unsaying—or kept in suspension (Sells, 1994; Webb and Sells, 1995).

2. Eigen (1981, 1985) discusses Bion's metapsychological use of Faith in psychoanalysis.

3. Bion's "use" of obscuration has much in common with current radiological and imaging techniques that seek to render large aspects of the visual field obscure so that the center can become all the more visible.

4. It is curious how, in autism, we associate the mechanism of "dismantling" of the image of the object and arrogating it to the control of the sense organs (Meltzer et al., 1975; Tustin, 1988) and not realize, except for Bion, that that is almost exactly what observational science, including psychoanalysis, has done since its inception.

5. Eigen (1995a, 1995b, 1995c) examines Bion's use of the concept of "no-thing."

6. I place a question mark (?) between the term "inner world" because of the belief, first adumbrated by Lacan (1966) that the Unconscious and its Subject are transpersonal phenomena since it is "structured like a language," and, according to Klein (1946, 1955) resides as projective identifications confused in the world at large of external objects.

7. I am indebted to Dr. Elizabeth Tabak de Bianchedi (1993) for her insightful explorations into Bion's conception of Truth.

8. I am indebted to Mrs. Edna O'Shaughnessy (1995) for her penetrating examination of Bion's conception of lies and -K phenomena.

9. Here I can only allude to the profundity of the ramifications of this point. Thinking, as associated with the ego, is ultimately associated with Column 2 of Bion's Grid, a designation of saturation that challenges the "messiah thought" inherent in the definitory hypothesis. If truth does not require a thinker, whereas lies, falsities, and even phantasies and conceptions do require a thinker, then who originally

and fundamentally "thinks" the unthought thoughts if not a profounder Presence within?

10. For an in-depth study of Bion's use of formal logic in psychoanalysis, see Skelton (1990, 1995).

11. My reading of Bion suggests that he makes a distinction between "virginal" beta elements, which exist prior to alpha functioning, and beta "rime" elements that have already had the door of alpha function "slammed in their face," so to speak.

12. From the Theurgic Kabbala of Zohar.

13. Electroencephalographically, this trance state of quiet wakefulness is associated with *theta rhythm*.

14. The italics are mine.

15. The italics are mine.

16. Italics are in the original text.

17. Italics by Ricoeur.

18. My italics.

19. My italics.

20. "Bad Object."

21. "Good Object."

22. I am indebted to Drssa. Parthenope Bion (personal communication, 1995) for her suggestion of "Wisdom."

23. See also Meltzer (1978, 1980, 1985) and the Symingtons (1996) for their readings of Bion's (1975, 1977b, 1979) *Memoir of the Future*.

24. When Bion was informed that he was dying of acute leukemia, he not uncharacteristically responded, "Life is full of surprises, all of them unpleasant!"

REFERENCES

Bianchedi, E. T. de (1993). Lies and falsities. *M. Klein Object Rel.*, 11(2):30-46.
Bion, W.R. (1959). Attacks on linking. In: *Second Thoughts*. London: Heinemann, 1967, pp. 93-109.
—— (1962). *Learning from Experience*. London: Heinemann.
—— (1963). *Elements of Psycho-Analysis*. London: Heinemann.
—— (1965). *Transformations*. London: Heinemann.
—— (1967). *Second Thoughts*. London: Heinemann.
—— (1970). *Attention and Interpretation*. London: Tavistock Pubns.
—— (1975). *A Memoir of the Future. Book I: The Dream*. Rio de Janeiro, Brazil: Imago Editora, Ltd.
—— (1977a). *Two Papers: The Grid and the Caesura*. Ed. Jayme Salomão. Rio de Janeiro: Imago Editora, Ltd.
—— (1977b). *A Memoir of the Future. Book II: The Past Presented*. Rio de Janeiro: Imago

Editora, Ltd.

Bion, W.R. (1979). *A Memoir of the Future. Book III: The Dawn of Oblivion*. Perthshire: Clunie Press.

—— (1982). *The Long Week-end 1897-1919: Part of a Life*. Ed. Francesca Bion. Abingdon: Fleetwood Press.

—— (1985). *All My Sins Remembered: Another Part of Life* and *The Other Side of Genius: Family Letters*. Ed. Francesca Bion. Abingdon: Fleetwood Press.

—— (1992). *Cogitations*. London: Karnac Books.

Blake, W. (1789-1794). *Songs of Innocence and Experience*. Oxford: Oxford University Press.

Bléandonu, G. (1994). *Wilfred Bion: His Life and Work. 1897-1979*. Translated by Claire Pajaczowska. London: Free Association Books.

Bloom, H. (1983). *Kabbalah and Criticism*. New York: Continuum.

Dehing, J. (1993). The transcendent function: A critical re-evaluation. In: *The Transcendent Function: Individual and Collective Aspects: Proceedings of The Twelfth International Congress for Analytical Psychology, Chicago, 1992*. Einssiedeln: Daimon Verlag, pp. 15-30.

Eigen, M. (1981). The area of faith in Winnicott, Lacan, and Bion. *Int. J. Psycho-Anal.*, 62: 413-434.

—— (1985). Towards Bion's starting point: Between catastrophe and faith. *Int. J. Psycho-Anal.*, 66: 321-330.

—— (1995a). On Bion's nothing. *M. Klein Obj. Rel.*, 13: 31-36.

—— (1995b). Moral violence: Space, time, causality, definition. *M. Klein Obj. Rel.*, 13: 37-45.

—— (1995c). Two kinds of no-thing. *M. Klein Obj. Rel.*, 13: 46-64.

Eliot, T.S. (1930). The love song of J. Alfred Prufrock. In: *The Wasteland and Other Poems*. New York & London: Harvest/Harcourt Brace Jovanovich, 1962, pp. 1-10.

—— (1943). Little gidding. In: *T.S. Eliot: Four Quartets*. San Diego, New York and London: Harvest/Harcourt Brace Jovanovich, 1971, pp. 49-59.

Fox, M. (1980). *Breakthrough: Meister Eckhart's Creation Spirituality in New Translation*. New York: Image (Doubleday).

—— (1981). Meister Eckhart on the fourfold path of a creation-centered spiritual journey. In: Fox, M. (Ed.), *Western Spirituality: Historical Roots, Ecumenical Routes*. Santa Fe, NM: Bear and Co., pp. 215-248.

Freud, S. (1900). *The Interpretation of Dreams. S. E.*, 1953, 5:339-630. In: J. Strachey (Ed.), *Standard Edition of the Complete Psychological Works of Sigmund Freud*, 24 volumes. London: Hogarth Press and The Institute of Psycho-Analysis, 1953-1974.

—— (1905). Jokes and their relationship to the unconscious. *S. E.*, 1960, 8:3-23.

—— (1911). Formulations of the two principles of mental functioning. *S. E.*, 1958,

12:213-226.

Freud, S. (1915). The unconscious. *S. E.*, 1957, 14: 159-215.

—— (1917). Mourning and melancholia. *S. E.*, 1957, 14: 237-260.

—— (1920). *Beyond the Pleasure Principle. S. E.*, 1955, 18: 3-66.

—— (1923). *The Ego and the Id. S. E.*, 1961, 19:3-59.

Freud, S. and Andreas-Salomé, L. (1966). Letter dated "25.5.16." In: Ernest Pfeiffer (Ed.), *Letters*. Translated by William and Elaine Robson-Scott. London: Hogarth Press, 1972, p. 45.

Frye, N. (1947). *Fearful Symmetry: A Study of William Blake*. Princeton, NJ: Princeton University Press.

Green, A. (1992). Book review: *Cogitations* by Wilfred R. Bion. *Int. J. Psycho-Anal.*, 73, 585-589.

Grotstein, J. (1978). Inner space: Its dimensions and its coordinates. *Int. J. Psycho-Anal.*, 59: 55-61.

—— (1981a). Bion the man, the psychoanalyst, and the mystic: A perspective on his life and work. In: J.S. Grotstein (Ed.), *Do I Dare Disturb the Universe? A Memorial to Wilfred R. Bion*. Beverly Hills, CA: Caesura, 1981, pp. 1-36.

—— (1981b). Who is the dreamer who dreams the dream, and who is the dreamer who understands it? In: J.S. Grotstein (Ed.), *Do I dare Disturb the Universe? A Memorial to Wilfred R. Bion*, pp. 357-416.

—— (1984). An odyssey into the deep and formless infinite: The work of Wilfred Bion. In: J. Reppen (Ed.), *Beyond Freud: A Study of Modern Psychoanalytic Theorists*. Hillsadle, NJ: Analytic Press, pp. 293-309.

—— (1990). The "black hole" as the basic psychotic experience: Some newer psychoanalytic and neuroscience perspectives on psychosis. *J. Amer. Acad. Psychoanal.*, 18(1): 29-46.

—— (1993). Towards the concept of the transcendent position: Reflections on some of "the unborns" in Bion's *Cogitations*. A contribution in the Special Issue on "Understanding the work of Wilfred Bion" for *M. Klein Obj. Rel.*, 11(2): 55-73.

—— (1995a). Orphans of the "Real": I. Some modern and post-modern perspectives on the neurobiological and psychosocial dimensions of psychosis and primitive mental disorders. *Bul. Men. Clinic*, 59: 287-311.

—— (1995b). Orphans of the "Real": II. The future of object relations theory in the treatment of psychoses and other primitive mental disorders. *Bul. Men. Clinic*, 59: 312-332.

Heidegger, M. (1931). *Being and time*. Translated by John Macquarrie and Edward Robinson. Third Edition. San Francisco: Harper Collins, 1962.

—— (1968). *The Metaphysical Foundations of Logic*. Translated by Michael Heim. Bloomington and Indianapolis: Indiana Universty Press.

Hofstadter, D. R. (1979). *Gödel, Escher, Bach: An Eternal Golden Braid*. New York: Basic Books.

Jung, C.G. (1916). *The Transcendent Function*. Translated by A.R. Pope. Privately printed for the Students' Association, C.G. Jung Institute, Zurich, 1957.
—— (1954). Transformation symbolism in the Mass. *Collected works*, 11: 203-296. Eighth Printing. London: Routledge & Kegan Paul, 1989.
Kant, I. (1787). *Critique of Pure Reason*. Translated by N. Kemp Smith. Second Edition. New York: St. Martin's Press, 1965.
Klein, M. (1933). The early development of conscience in the child. In: *Contributions to Psycho-Analysis, 1921-1945*. London: Hogarth Press, 1950, pp. 267-277.
—— (1935). A contribution to the psychogenesis of manic-depressive states. In: *Contributions to Psycho-Analysis, 1921-1945*, pp. 282-310.
—— (1940). Mourning and its relation to manic depressive states. In: *Contributions to Psycho-Analysis, 1921-1945*, pp. 344-369.
—— (1946). Notes on some schizoid mechanisms. *The Writings of Melanie Klein*. London: Hogarth Press, vol. 3, pp. 1-24.
—— (1955). The psycho-analytic play technique: Itshistory and significance. *The Writings of Melanie Klein*, vol. 3, pp. 122-140.
Lacan, J. (1966). *Écrits*. Paris: Seuil. Re-published: *Écrits: 1949-1960*. Translated by A. Sheridan. New York: W.W. Norton, 1977.
Matte-Blanco, I. (1975). *The Unconscious as Infinite Sets*. London: Duckworth.
—— (1988). *Thinking, Feeling, and Being: Clinical Reflections on the Fundamental Antinomy of Human Beings*. London & New York: Tavistock and Routledge.
Meltzer, D. (1978). *The Kleinian Development. Part III. The Clinical Significance of the Work of Bion*. Perthshire: Clunie Press.
—— (1980). "The diameter of the circle" in Wilfred Bion's work. In: A. Hahn (Ed.), *Sincerity and Other Works: Collected Papers of Donald Meltzer*. London: Karnac Books, 1994, pp. 469-474.
—— (1985) (with Meg Harris Williams). Three lectures on W.R. Bion's *A Memoir of the Future*. In: A. Hahn (Ed.), *Sincerity and Other Works: Collected Papers of Donald Meltzer*, pp. 520-550.
Meltzer, D.W., Bremner, J., Hoxter, S., Wedell, H., Wittenberg, I. (1975). *Explorations in autism*. Perthshire: Clunie Press.
Milton, J. (1667). Paradise Lost. In: E. Le Comte (Ed.) *Paradise Lost and Other Poems*. New York: Mentor, 1961, pp. 33-344.
Moore, A.W. (1995). A brief history of infinity. *Scientific American*, April, pp. 112-116.
Nietzsche, F. (1883). *Thus spoke Zarathustra*. Translated by R.J. Hollingdale. Penguin, 1969.
O'Shaughnessy, E. (1995). Minus K. Presented at the Panel "Bion's Contribution to Psychoanlytic Theory and Technique" at the 39th International Psychoanalytic Conference in San Francisco, CA on Monday, July 31, 1995.
Pagels, E. (1979). *The Gnostic Gospels*. New York: Vintage Press.

Rayner, E. (1995). *Unconscious Logic: An Introduction to Matte Blanco's Bi-Logic and its Uses*. London & New York: Routledge.

Rayner, E. & Tuckett, D. (1988). An introduction to Matte-Blanco's reformulation of the Freudian unconscious and his conceptualization of the internal world. In: Matte-Blanco, I. (1988). *Thinking, Feeling, and Being*. London & New York: Routledge, pp. 3-42.

Ricoeur, P. (1970). *Freud and Philosophy: An Essay on Interpretation*. Translated by Denis Savage. New Haven, CT & London: Yale University Press.

Samuels, A., Shorter, B., Plaut, F. (1986). *A Critical Dictionary of Jungian Analysis*. London & New York: Routledge.

Scholem, G. G. (1969). *The Kabbalah and its Symbolism*. Translated by Ralph Manheim. New York: Schocken.

Segal, H. (1957). Notes on symbol formation. *Int. J. Psycho-Anal.*, 38: 391-397.

—— (1981). Notes on symbol formation. In: *The Work of Hanna Segal: A Kleinian Approach to Clinical Practice*. New York & London: Jason Aronson, pp. 49-68.

Sells, M.A. (1994). *The Mystical Language of Unsaying*. Chicago & London: University of Chicago Press.

Skelton, R. (1990). Generalization from Freud to Matte-Blanco. *Int. Rev. Psycho-Anal.*, 17: 471-474.

—— (1995). Bion's use of modern logic. *Int. J. Psycho-Anal.*, 76: 389-397.

Solomon, H. (1994). The transcendent function and Hegel's dialectical vision. *J. Anal. Psychol.*, 39: 77-100.

Symington, J., Symington, N. (1996). *The Clinical Thinking of Wilfred Bion*. London & New York: Routledge. In press.

Tustin, F. (1988). The "black hole"—A significant element in autism. *Free Assns.*, 11: 35-50.

Webb, R.E., Sells, M.A. (1995). Lacan and Bion: Psychoanalysis and the mystical language of "unsaying." *Theory Psychol.* In press.

Williams, M.H. (1985). The tiger and "O": A reading of Bion's *Memoir of the future*. *Free Assns.*, 1: 33-56.

Winnicott, D.W. (1988). Chaos. In: *Human Nature*. London: Free Association Books, pp. 135-138.

Wittgenstein, L. (1933-1935). *The Blue and Brown Books*. New York: Harper & Row, 1958.

522 Dalehurst Avenue
Los Angeles, California 90024
USA

JOURNAL OF MELANIE KLEIN AND OBJECT RELATIONS
Vol. 14, No. 2, December 1996

CALL FOR PAPERS

The Journal of Melanie Klein and Object Relations cordially invites authors to submit papers for the following Special Issues:

THE PSYCHO-ANALYTIC PROCESS BY D. MELTZER: 30 YEARS LATER

PSYCHOANALYTIC PERSPECTIVES ON HATE

Contributors are invited to send immediately a brief letter of interest, the title of the paper and a summary of maximum 250 words. Send manuscripts to the Editor by *September 1, 1997*. All manuscripts should conform to the style of this publication (see "Instructions to Authors"). Proposals for other topics for Special Issues are welcomed, as well.

* * *

CALL FOR BOOK AND FILM REVIEWS

The *Journal of Melanie Klein and Object Relations* is accepting book and film reviews, and reviews of several books in the form of essays. Send manuscripts to the Editor. All manuscripts should conform to the style of this publication (see "Instructions for Authors").

WORKING-THROUGH, OR BEYOND THE DEPRESSIVE POSITION? (ACHIEVEMENTS AND DEFENSES OF THE SPIRITUAL POSITION, AND THE HEART'S CONTENT)

Neil Maizels

The author explores some conceptual and technical issues in relation to the terms "Depressive Position" and "the Working-Through of the Depressive Position," and in so doing, suggests a new concept—"the Spiritual Position." It is proposed that this spiritual position has achievements, such as a capacity for "meta feeling," ∫, and defenses, which are somewhat different, although related to the mourning and reparation of the working-through of the depressive position. Particular attention is paid to the development of the "whole-object Father" in the formation of an "observing-ego-in-feeling," and to the development of the "whole-object Mother" (Nature) in the formation of a "meta-morphosic," feeling, philosophy of Life. Together, these formations give the mind a "heart," which may come under attack from an omniscient, Tiresias-like internal object. Some clinical material is used to illustrate these achievements and defenses, and to highlight the difference of emphasis (as compared with the working-through of the depressive position) that they imply.

> Low lie the mists; they hide each hill and dell
> The grey skies weep with us who bid farewell
> But happier days through memory weaves a spell
> And brings new hope to hearts who bid farewell.
>
> (Charles E. Ives, 1925 edition)

> Science will not trust us with another World.
>
> (Emily Dickinson, 1993 edition)

In Melanie Klein's *Narrative of a Child Analysis* (1961) there is, to me, a very puzzling moment where both child and analyst are struggling to understand what it is to have a "heart." The analysis is accelerating, somewhat tragically, towards termination, and Richard is discussing his "Lovely Mrs. Klein" drawing.

> Mrs. K. interpreted Richard's struggle between his loving and hating her. He was trying to think that she was nice; beside the drawing representing her at the top of the page he had written "lovely Mrs. K." Nevertheless, he did not actually think that she was lovely, and therefore drew her without arms and hair, and evidently had no intention of making her look nice. He hated her for leaving him and joining other patients and her son and grandson. Richard insisted that Mrs. K. was lovely on the drawing because her tummy was heart-shaped and the arrow in the middle of it meant love. (His face was flushed and he often put his finger into his mouth; the struggle between hate and the wish to control it, and the mixture of persecutory and depressive anxiety, were expressed on his face.) He asked whether Mrs. K. was sorry to go away. Was she going to stay with her son? She was not going to live in the heart of London was she? Richard suddenly became aware of the word "heart," look surprised, and pointing at the drawing said, "But here is the heart." Mrs. K. interpreted that her heart stood for the bombed London and was *not only injured by love (the arrow)* but also by bombs. Richard, who wished to love Mrs. K., was afraid that, because she was leaving him, he might turn into Hitler who was going to bomb her. This increased his fear of her death, his loneliness, and his sadness about her departure. (pp. 412-413)

But what does Klein mean by "injured by love"?

Quite clearly she is trying to convey to Richard, in emotional terms, her theory of the depressive position. That is, to bring to his awareness the struggle between love and hate within his mind, and his difficulties in holding both feelings towards the one object.

Richard seems to be saying:

> I am trying to find something symbolic which will convey my struggle to love you in spite of feeling injured by your leaving me to be with others. And this symbol, to my surprise, brings together feelings about your tummy, your other sons, and the place you are going to, in the form of a wounded heart.

This paper will briefly trace some of the complications of the Kleinian terms "depressive position" and "working-through of the depressive position," and will explore the usefulness of the "old-fashioned" notion of having a "heart." The aim is dual, in that I will not only present a way of clarifying, but also of extending these concepts. My reasons for attempting such difficult tasks is that I have grown increasingly dissatisfied with the enormous burden which these terms bear for those who have found value in Klein's work. So I will attempt to explore the issue of whether or not Klein's conception of the "working-through of the depressive position" is adequately differentiated from the "achievement of the depressive position," and further, whether or not the former is still adequate for our current understanding of the farther reaches of emotional development. Whether or not these clarifications and extensions are actually more useful clinically than the current conceptions of the depressive position and the working-through of the depressive position is hard to determine, partly because, unfortunately, almost all "postdepressive" emotional development has, in my view, all too easily been sheltering under the umbrella term depressive position.

A clinical illustration will be given as an indication of why I have found it worthwhile to consider some changes to the concepts.

One of the major difficulties inherent in the writing of a paper about the process of emotional integration in development is that one needs to speak of many different things at once, and from different points of view. So my argument will be put more like the branches of a tree rather than linearly, in the hope that its somewhat intangible "trunk" might be revealed implicitly.

The Depressive Position

It is not possible, in this paper, to give a complete history of the different shades of meaning that the term "depressive position" has accumulated since Melanie Klein's naming of "it." Good summaries have been provided by Segal (1964) and Hinshelwood (1989), among others, and although I will underline some aspects of these definitions, I mainly want to show some of the conceptual "indefiniteness" that has accompanied "postdepressive" emotional growth. Meltzer (1978, p. 114) has noted an array of meanings indicated by terms such as overcoming, surpassing and penetrating the depressive position, where previously the term "working-through the depressive position" was more common, and he himself uses the term "threshold of the depressive position" where previously the term "achievement of the depressive position" was more common. In fact we use the latter term rather than say "the working-through of the paranoid-schizoid position." Yet we do not have a term for something new achieved by the working-through of the depressive position. (Perhaps the term which I used above, that is, "postdepressive" is the closest there is to such a term, although some nontechnical terms such as mature ambivalence or mature concern have sometimes been used.)

I think that there are at least two reasons why the working-through of depressive anxieties has not been given a distinctive new name.

The first reason is that many analysts feel that "the depressive position is never fully worked through" (Segal, 1964, p. 74). This is the belief that emotional growth consists of the *ongoing, lifelong* struggle to move from part-object, preambivalent, persecutory states of mind to whole-object, ambivalent, concerned states of mind, with some increasing confidence that love for one's good objects can, on the whole, ameliorate or repair one's destructive intentions to them.

> The whole relationship to objects alters as the depressive position is gradually worked through. The infant acquires the capacity to love and respect people as separate, differentiated individuals. He becomes capable of acknowledging his impulses, of feeling a sense of responsibility for them and of tolerating guilt. The new capacity to feel concern for his objects helps him to learn gradually to control his impulses. (Segal, 1964, p. 74)

The other reason for no new term seems to be that *all* emotional integration and creativity are attributed to the working-through of the depressive position.

> The infant's longing to recreate his lost objects gives him the impulse to put together what has been torn asunder, to reconstruct what has been destroyed, to recreate and to create. At the same time, his wish to spare his objects leads him to sublimate his impulses when they are felt to be destructive. Thus, his concern for his object modifies his instinctual aims and brings about an inhibition of instinctual drives. (Segal, 1964, p. 75)

Segal then equates all creative, artistic and particularly symbolic mental work with this working-through of the depressive position. The strength of her approach has been to bring a new "test" of emotional depth to creative endeavors. But this, in my view, has also been a drawback, often giving the "thumbs down" to works of art and states of mind which do not appear to be primarily concerned with the working-through of the depressive position, or, more specifically, with reparative intentions towards internal damaged objects through concerned guilt.

I want to explore the idea that it may be useful *not* to group all types of emotionally integrative states under the "banner" of working-through the depressive position, although I acknowledge that it is certainly possible, and often helpful, to do this.

I perceive a state of emotional perception and transformation which, although absolutely dependent on capacities such as concern (and gratitude) for the maternal object as separate and with needs and a mind of her own, i.e., the "working-through of the depressive position," carries qualities of mind more usefully kept distinct.

Such emotional states seem to have a level of integrity, dream language, and depth of feeling, together with defenses against the depth of feeling, all of their own. I will try to argue that a new conception and vocabulary for this—what I will refer to as "the spiritual position"—might be of use clinically, and might also help to unravel some knotted metapsychological issues which are gradually becoming more apparent within that body of clinicians who make use of Melanie Klein's work.

"Transpersonal" psychologists (such as Assagnini, Groff, or Maslow) have addressed the importance of "spiritual growth" and "metareflection," but I hope to give more intrapsychic detail than their paradigms have, in my view, allowed.

Working-Through of the Depressive Position and Catastrophic Change

Perhaps I can briefly illustrate the stretch and strain that seem to be evolving between "Kleinian" and "Post-Kleinian" along the theoretical ridge where "depressive position," "working-through of the depressive position," "threshold of the depressive position" and Bion's "catastrophic change" vie, by giving two examples.

The first example consists of some critical comments made by Kate Barrows (1993) in her review of the "post-Kleinian" book *The Chamber of Maiden Thought. Literary Origins of the Psychoanalytic Model of the Mind* (Harris-Williams and Waddell, 1991).

The "Chamber of Maiden Thought" seems to represent a place in the mind where not knowing can be tolerated and where there is an intense aesthetic experience as well as increased awareness of dark or painful feelings.

(but)

... the concept of unconscious guilt frequently seems to be missing in the accounts of literary works; hence awareness of damage to internal objects and the importance of reparation in the creative processes are often surprisingly absent. (p. 208)

Klein suggested that the creative process arises from a wish to restore damaged internal objects; this understanding led to her subsequent formulation of the concept of the depressive position. (p. 209)

(but)

... instead of awareness of depressive pain and ambivalence, idealized parental figures, or "deities," are often invoked by the authors. It is this tendency to idealization which seems to obviate the need for recognition of the role of responsibility for unconscious guilt and the importance of feelings of compassion and concern in the transition from omnipotence to the depressive position. (p. 208)

So, whereas Harris-Williams and Waddell stress the importance of the internalized combined parents as forming a super (Platonic) ego-ideal, Barrows sees this model as a clinging to idealized (that is, part-object) parents.

Although a simple resolution of the differences of perspective does not seem possible, or even desirable, I will try to bring them closer together later in this paper through some clinical material. (I have made some further comments on the difference between the Klein/Segal depressive-reparative model of creativity and the Bion/Meltzer/Harris-Williams catastrophic change-through-inspiring-ego-ideal model elsewhere [Maizels, 1994]).

A second example of slips of meaning when using the depressive position terminology is apparent in the following comments by Hinshelwood (1989) on Grotstein's supposed misunderstanding of the term—that is, of Grotstein's supposed confusion between depressive anxiety and the working-through of the depressive position.

Depressive anxiety: The crucial feature of the depressive position, the anguishing over the state of the object, was criticized from a self-psychology point of view by Grotstein (1983):

Klein has placed too much emphasis on the welfare of the object by the infant and has seemingly sacrificed the right of the infant to have a "self" of his or her own and/or to have recognition of the self's needs independent of consideration of the object's welfare (p. 529).

However, what he is describing is exactly the pain of the depressive position in its early stages when the guilt has a strongly persecutory tone that demands extreme self-sacrifice and slavery. It is because of this developmentally early quality to depressive anxiety that the person evades it, defends against it or retreats to the paranoid-schizoid position. It is only by working-through this that the infant and older individuals can come to an easier adjustment between their concern for their object and the normal degree of self-respect (a sort of normal narcissism) required to look after themselves (see Rosenfeld). (pp. 152-153)

In spite of Hinshelwood's criticism, Grotstein (1993) actually prefers a different term of his own for growth "beyond" the depressive position—when it is worked through. He calls this the "transcendent position" which he sees as bringing serenity through a sense of "ultimate reality" (Bion's "O") which nonetheless rests on adequate mourning processes. (This seems similar to Jacques (1965) conception of the working-through of the depressive position as "sculpting creativity" in the service of a serene philosophical emotional achievement.) He therefore locates the experience of catastrophic change to somewhere beyond the "working-through of the depressive position," whereas Meltzer (1978) and Eric Rhode (1987) locate such "catastrophic" emotional movement (quivering between Ps and D) at the "threshold" of the depressive position.

But in the light of the above crossing of definition, could they (Meltzer and Rhode) mean the threshold of the *working-through* of the depressive position? At this threshold, change of one's emotional values is feared as a catastrophe, which has two, related but distinctive components.

1. The onslaught of *seemingly* unbearable guilt.
2. Fear of the loss involved in the transformation of the self, into a new person, through a "change of heart."

In my conception of a "spiritual position," catastrophic change becomes an ironic term, as the self becomes open to transformation and metamorphosis, and this enables and inspires one to have feelings about life, with all its vicissitudes and unending change. (Without this, one cannot experience what the Germans call *Vergangenheitsbewältigung*—a feeling of coming to terms with one's past— and without that, one cannot come to terms with the concept of death.)

Beyond the Depressive Position

I will now describe the particular characteristics of the "spiritual position," together with defenses against it, then some case material and more detailed discussion will follow, where I will make some attempt to resolve some of the theoretical issues mentioned above.

I suggest that there is a level of "meta"-feeling in the spiritual position, where one has *feelings about* one's accumulated feelings (∫).

In a sense this model resembles Shelley's (1967 edition) poetic images of the growth of mind, where accumulations (clouds) of pining feelings are let flow into the accumulations of loving remembrances. This "spiritual" state, where one has feelings about all the feelings that one has experienced, feelings about life, *may* be serene, but not necessarily. The poignancy and plangency of the spiritual position gives it an emotional fluidity perhaps similar to the function of music to film images. ∫ gives a kind of reverse barometer reading, emotionally, in that it reads the atmosphere that has accumulated rather than that which is gathering.

It may well involve a simultaneous emotional perception of love and hate being brought together towards the one object, in the Kleinian sense of ambivalence. But it involves a level of "emotional abstraction" whereby the "whole-object" is felt, beyond the parental, to be life (or God). Catastrophic change is therefore the catastrophic annihilation of the part-object mother in order to make her more whole; that is, more in keeping with the whole truth of one's feelings towards her.

Defenses Against the Spiritual Position

Part of my attempt to differentiate this spiritual position is to describe emotional defenses which seem different in quality and content to the manic defenses of the depressive position. (See Segal, 1964, pp. 95-96.) This is not an easy matter.

While the latter defensive system centers around the avoidance of guilt, concern, and the need to repair the internal good object caused by one's destructive intentions, the following defenses of the spiritual position are more to do with the avoidance of feelings towards the repaired, fully-functioning, whole-object, when it is able to grip one's "heart" and bring about constantly metamorphic changes in the self, over which one has very limited control.

These defenses may seem similar to some manic or obsessional defenses of the depressive position, but here they are present *together with* a capacity for genuine concern and guilt (which is not present in manic or obsessive manoeuvres).

Briefly, the defenses are:

1. An obsession with security and habit, repeating only what is "tried and true," and "proving" the propaganda that only what is tried can be true. This keeps "at bay" the emotional realization that "... only the truest things always are true because they can't be true" (E.E. Cummings, 1958). Therefore the tide (of change) can never be taken "at the flood." Or, at the opposite extreme, change is brought about in a manic frenzy in order to give the illusion of control of all change, and to keep its emotional impact "un-new," and un-inspiring—an addiction to catastrophe, as opposed to the allowing of "catastrophic change." This amounts to a denial of mystery and illogicality as an unmistakable presence in one's life experiences.

2. Depression is adhered to by repeated futile attempts to "repair" the "old" mother to continuously restore her, rather than to take the helm of the mind's ship and move out into the deep unknown of oneself, as captured in Whitman's "The Explorers":

   Oh, we can wait no longer...
   we too launch out on trackless seas,
   ... sail forth, steer for the deep waters only....

   and at the same time, to see other qualities in the object apart from good or bad, frustrating or gratifying.

3. Identification used as a defense against dis-identification. By this I mean to include resistances against the extremely painful (but liberating) mental act of relinquishing (perhaps even renouncing) one's allegiance, ego-syntonicity and identification with a previously-helpful and relevant good internal object which is no longer such to the emerging *new-born* self. This work usually begins, very tentatively, in the termination phase of analysis or psychotherapy, but continues on well beyond it.

4. Hysterical precedence given to "feeling" as compared to feelings *about* feelings, so that depth and "perspective" never build in the personality. (Britton [1989], Fullerton [1994], and Young [1994] have linked the acceptance of the Oedipal Couple by the infant, in the

depressive position, with the ability to gain a "third-person" perspective—a kind of detached observer mental stance, in order to
reflect.) Here, included as a defense against the Spiritual Position, I
am emphasizing the resistance to meta-feeling per se, in the "heart of
the mind."

5. The obsessive activity of trying to change other people, to avoid
change in oneself, and to remain unknowing of how one really feels
about the reality of other people as they are.

6. A "flatulent" juxtaposition of one's life events in emotional memory,
as compared with a creative recombinatory revisiting-for-the-first
time from new insight and perspective—perhaps what George Uloid
(Waddell, 1986) would call "fresh and fresh wholes." (A patient
continued to paste a deadening "it's just like..." onto my attempts to
make lively interpretations. But these forced juxtapositions inevitably
ground free associations to a halt.)

7. A flight from the *"shock of the repaired."* This manifests in a stubborn
and fearful refusal to accept the "death" of the old in the constant
regeneration of the new—what Ovid (1986 edition) illustrated so
vividly in his collage of stories of human transformation entitled
Metamorphoses. In the depressive position, emotional acceptance of the
whole-object mother contains the "death" of the part-object mother.
But there is a difficulty in accepting the *transformed* and *transforming*
aspects of the new, repaired object.
   The endings of Shakespeare's *The Winter's Tale* and Hemingway's *For
Whom the Bell Tolls,* exemplify this struggle in the "spiritual position,"
while *King Lear* and Alfred Hitchcock's *Vertigo* move us to feel the
tragic consequences of literal "reparation" preventing transfigura-
tional loss and regeneration—where the "hero" cannot let his loved
object "become" herself, but imposes his own limited stereotype on
to her personality.

Depressive loss is only borne and transcended with the acceptance of
(perhaps even rejoicing in) the *metamorphic spirit* of life—where regeneration
is *never* exactly the same as the "old" which has run its course and been lost
in its tomb of absolute uniqueness.

The defense can manifest itself in an obsession with "fixing" (with its
double meaning!) things—to keep them untransformed. This sort of
reparation is a defense against letting the object develop into something

different and *new*. It has a different quality and intention to it than Klein's mock or manic reparation.

An asthmatic patient dreamt that she was whacking her mother in the head, but the mother kept changing form, so the patient had to whack her again and again until she (the patient) became paralysed and "hysterical". (Eric Rhode [1987] notes that hysteria is all about one's feelings about "changing form.")

The best description that I can find, at present, for the "home" in the mind for the "reverse barometer" of the spiritual position, is the old-fashioned term "heart," which must be continuously informed by what I would call the observing-ego-in-feeling.

But the difficulty and emotional strain of maintaining the spiritual position for very long before it cracks into pessimism or an aloof "philosophical shield" is disturbingly registered by Dostoyevsky (1871) in *The Devils*:

> There are seconds—they come five or six at a time—when you suddenly feel the presence of external harmony in all its fullness. It is nothing earthly. I don't mean that it is heavenly, but a man in his earthly semblance can't endure it. He has to undergo a change or die. The feeling is clear and unmistakable. It is as though you suddenly apprehended all nature and suddenly said: "Yes, it is true—it is good... It is not rapture, but just gladness... What is so terrifying about it is that it is so terribly clear and such gladness. If it went on for more than five seconds, the soul could not endure it and must perish. (p. 586)

The miraculous human capacity to risk "having a heart" throughout all one's life is virtually impossible, given that one is always risking the loss of all that one loves and knows—unless one's heart is "tuned," over time, to the metamorphic spirit of transfigural regeneration. But more often, even in the working-through of the depressive position, one's "heart" is in identification with a painful, bleeding breast—wounded in love.

In Shelley's (1967) poem *Epipsychidion*, the lines:

> High, spirit-winged Heart! who doest for ever
> Beat thine unfeeling bars with vain endeavour,
> 'Till those bright plumes of thought, in which arrayed
> It over-soared this low and worldly shade,
> Lie shattered; and thy panting, wounded breast
> Stains with dear blood its unmaternal nest!
> I weep vain tears: blood would less bitter be,

Yet poured forth gladlier, could it profit thee.

seem to express the heart's agony in the emotional presence of the re-
unified, repaired loved one, evoked in:

> ... And from her presence life was radiated
> Through the grey earth and branches bare and dead;
> So that her way was paved, and roofed above
> With flowers as soft as thoughts of budding love;
> And music from her respiration spread
> Like light, —all other sounds were penetrated
> By the small, still, sweet spirit of that sound,
> So that the savage winds hung mute around;
> And odours warm and fresh fell from her hair
> Dissolving the dull cold in the frore air:
> Soft as an Incarnation of the Sun,
> When light is changed to love, this glorious One
> Floated into the cavern where I lay,
> And called my Spirit, and the dreaming clay
> Was lifted by the thing that dreamed below
> As smoked by fire, and in her beauty's glow
> I stood, and felt the dawn of my long night
> Was penetrating me with living light: .... (325-340)

I will now try to give more detail and clinical evidence for the spiritual
position and its defenses. This will also involve some elaboration of the
plangent, observing-ego-in-feeling in the formation of the "heart" of the
mind, and some evidence for the existence of an internal object whose aim
is "heart attack."

Case Material

Spillius (1994) gives a touching account of a patient's unconscious
reaction to termination of her analysis through a dream told by the patient
in her final session. In the dream the patient was strolling around, and
admiring, some particularly "primitive" countryside in New Zealand that
she had never seen before. But she gradually became aware that she could
not stay, and was saddened to have to leave the place. As she was leaving
she had to remind herself to be careful not to damage some particularly
beautiful blue trees.

The perspective that I am emphasizing would not understate the importance of the emotional acceptance of separation, loss, and the poignant development of a caring and responsible attitude regarding the damaging of unique good objects, which are allowed to retain mystery and left to be. (The analyst had been linked to New Zealand in the patient's mind.)

All of these achievements would be seen as the working-through of the depressive position. Nor would the perspective fail to notice the "test" of this working-through—passed with "flying colors"—in the patient's ability to symbolize difficult and sad emotional experience—in this case, the loss of her analytic sessions.

What the perspective of the spiritual position might bring to this fragment of material, is the appreciation of the patient's capacity to have feelings about her analysis, herself, and her life, on the whole.

A good part of the poignancy of the dream is that it carries feelings of admiration and loss of something that is now seen in very broad emotional perspective—like stepping back to view a whole canvas—and so the analysis as a whole emotional experience is installed as a place in her mind, inspiring reverence, awe and delicacy.

Moving, in a sense, "backwards" from this example, I will now present a more detailed account of what I see as the psychological evolution of this capacity for having feelings about one's life experience "as a whole."

I will try to show this as intimately related to a postdepressive, emotional ability to maintain an intact "heart"; and by this I refer to the old-fashioned concept of the heart as the center for intuitive, but genuine perception of feeling in the personality as a whole. Therefore the "workings" of the heart remain essentially mysterious and therefore unconscious, although its feeling sensibility is often available through what I shall call "the observing-ego-in feeling." I will elaborate on this concept after the clinical example.

The case presented here is extremely clipped and shorn of many of its transferential details in order to highlight particular thematic strands and their development, where this is relevant to my topic of postdepressive emotional capacities—particularly this capacity to maintain a whole functioning "heart."

The patient "arrived" for treatment in an unnervingly dishevelled manner— saying that she had heard of me, but couldn't quite remember how, and that most probably she needed help because her life was in a mess. She had arrived in Australia only a few months prior to seeking treatment, and she could see that her move was both an escape from increasingly chaotic liaisons with dangerous, but, to her, sexually attractive men, and also an attempt to "change herself." She expressed doubts about her choice of career as a Social Worker; partly because it provided too much opportunity for entanglements with highly disturbed men, and partly because it felt too much her mother's choice of career for her, rather than following her own inclinations and talents, which she located in the world of the Arts, particularly film. She had written five film scripts, but they had felt "stillborn" and she had not dared to show them to anyone.

In the initial sessions she presented as a kind of alluring "Tinker Bell" —not quite "womanly," but pervading an ambience of promising intimacy and budding love, which felt both enticing and suspicious; as if I should be very careful to curb my positive feelings towards her.

To put it another way; in the countertransference, I felt like a father who wishes to cuddle his daughter, but who stiffens up and feels safer being aloof for fear of inappropriate sexual feeling being stimulated in himself or the child, and this, of course, creates an even more charged atmosphere of *forbidden* (Oedipal) sensuality. Before long we could trace this field as, in some ways, a retreat from and a revenge on a very limited, depriving internal mother. (Often she would shop for milk before and after a session.) But in other ways this emotional field expressed a yearning for a lost, warm playfulness, where the vulnerable infant could feel held in father's lap and stroked by his gaze, consoled for her incomplete engagement of mother's body and mind.

The patient was the youngest of six daughters and felt that she had enjoyed a privileged intimacy with father until he died of a heart attack in her third year, following which she adopted the role of a Cinderella stuck at home with an insensitive mother and several ugly and stupid sisters.

A rapt attentiveness and responsiveness to my interpretations were peppered with a cool dismissiveness whenever I was felt to be (and felt myself to be) very close. Internally, there was a passionately, if intrusively, attached infant and a fickle, aloof parent. This internal coupling existed in a highly sadomasochistic state of game-playing and teasing, and was the basis of much of the "cockteasing" she had played at from teenagehood, but which was worrying to her in early adulthood.

As we were able to expose some of the cruelty involved in the constant projective identification away of the passionate, hungry infant in herself, she began to become horrified and eventually concerned about what this was doing to other people and to her own development. She began to recall teenage episodes with her girlfriends in cars, waving provocatively at boys, and then being both excited and shocked when the boys would give chase at high speeds, and she saw how intensely she could stir up sexual and aggressive feelings in them.

This disowning of her own passionate baby self showed in dreams where a vulnerable baby rabbit (a "bunny") was always left exposed and unprotected against the ravages of a stupid, ignorant dog or wolf. We could also link this to an aspect of her character which came to be called the "wolf in bunny's clothing"—"innocently" devouring the "hearts" of desperate young men.

In one session she was jolted by a slip she made while describing the temptation she had felt during the previous holiday break to play "funny buggers." Instead, she said "... to play bunny fuckers."

As she began to relinquish these unsatisfying projective identifications and experience more of the "wolfish" in herself, which wished to swallow all parental attention and intimacy for herself alone, she began to feel more kinship with her sisters in the struggle to live without a father. But she also began to feel less "stuck inside" her mother's supposed expectations regarding her career choices.

Complaints about my breaks were about how she couldn't enjoy what she wanted to do—expressed in a slip where she said that she felt compelled to have the "stranded" (she had meant to say "standard") break—and was stuck in a kind of depressive claustrophobia. But where this had previously been part of an intensely envious hatred of those whom she saw as free to "follow their own hearts," she now felt free to leave the "compulsive givers" (including that view of her therapist) and to pursue her screenwriting. She also pursued a man whom she had at first seen as "a jerk" but now experienced him as highly desirable and sincere. (In the transference, I was now experienced as having real feelings of my own, and even vulnerable to illness, accidents and financial struggle, so that my interest in helping her was no longer taken for granted.) In fact her career accelerated at a rapid pace soon after she showed her "stillborn" scripts (which had been kept as stillborn siblings in her internal world) to a "producer-friend" of this man, and, interestingly, nine months later, a new script was bought for a highly successful television drama series concerned with "rescue." She received some critical acclaim, two film commissions, and, for the first time, lived in a "place of her own."

At this time she brought a new openness to sessions, and was able to speak freely about habits she had which she found unattractive, and was not so compelled to always portray herself as the "cute bunny." One of these habits, she noticed, was a tendency to mindlessly shove bits of ice-cream wrappers into the crevices of her car seat as she was driving. The name of her favorite ice-cream, ("Heart") and other associations, suggested that these were unconscious attempts to push away and treat as rubbish her own heart-felt feelings of love and attachment. Such "habits" were a kind of masturbatory "cut-out circuit," for whenever she felt enough love to be risking the possibility of a "broken heart."

Sometimes, during breaks, they were enacted more destructively in flirtations with dangerous men, and were always lamented after the break with a back-of-hand-on-forehead castigation like "How could I let myself do that?" (If sometimes her self-castigation lacked sincerity, then at other times it seemed to lack compassion.)

But the approach to the fourth end-of-year break brought a dream which moved her deeply. After saying, somewhat facetiously, that the dream felt "too deep for tears" she began to cry as she told it.

At first she was immersed, up in the air somewhere, in a puffy, wet grey mist. It felt dull, heavy and very depressing. But gradually she was able to separate herself out from the wetness, and saw that she had been in a very large white cloud, which was in the perfect shape of a lamb. When she recognized this in the dream she felt calm and complete and relieved; as if something damaged inside her had been restored, and was working again.

Further work in the following sessions linked the lamb with lost lambent feelings (she had been playing with the word lambent in a poem) associated with memories in feeling of playing in father's lap, and this enabled her to recover some totally forgotten perceptions of her mother as a happy and secure person, prior to father's death. (Grinberg's, 1978, stressing of the importance of recovering the *parts of the self* associated to, or in relationship with, the good objects seems relevant here.)

Other associations to the dream cannot be included here, along with many other elements of the transference and vicissitudes of the patient's development. But I will conclude the case example by following one particularly prominent thematic strand which was gradually revealed to be central in her flight from "good" relationships.

This theme concerned the emotional struggle to "have a heart."

Although I have not made it explicit so far, the patient commenced in an intensely, if unconscious, suicidal state. The early, often-repeated dreams were of steep, hostile cliff faces, overlooking a cold, rough ocean. Often, in these dreams, she was falling, or wanting to fall onto the rocks below the cliff-faces, wishing to dash her heart against these rocks. As she developed some trust towards me, a man began to appear in these settings who was trying to both stop her from falling, and to take her out on a lifeboat towards a ship that would take her to warmer shores.

Some associational work suggested the obvious identification with the father who died from an "attacked" heart, but more particularly to a film which had saddened and heartened her. The film was *Papillon*, which depicted two prisoners trapped on a prison island, until one of them has the courage to jump into the sea and swim to freedom. She found it sad that the other companion was left behind forever. It was "heart-breaking."

In the session prior to an extended Christmas break, where she was to return to her native country to visit her unwell mother and also to visit the grave of her father for the first time, she brought this dream:

> She was alone in very rough weather, but a man with kind eyes and a lantern held her hand and led her to a helicopter which raised her upwards until she could see thousands and thousands of people similar to herself, even though it seemed to be night. This made her feel more human, and then the helicopter set her down near to a warm fire where "the rest of humanity" were gathered and murmuring in a reassuring way. She thanked the man, and asked him what his name was; and he said that he was "Arturo Sclerosa." This unsettled her, but the warmth from the fire drew her to stay.

Her associations were of arteriosclerosis, heart attacks, and feeling homeless; but Arturo the lantern holder must be Arturo Toscanini, she thought. But, she went on, Toscanini conducts with too much military passion, and not enough heart. Then she thought of Mahler as having too much heart. "Didn't he die of heart disease? Wasn't he too much in love with his wife who caused him heartbreak?"

But her thoughts about matters of the heart did not always seem to be coming from the heart. Or they sounded like statements about somebody else's feelings.

The next dream in the "heart series" gave us some further insight into the problem.

> An archaeological team were digging up the road in a "lost city"—there was a gaping hole in the road—heart-shaped—but you couldn't get close enough to get a really good look at the site because of "Keep Out" signs all around it.

Her associations were to the Sleeping Beauty, and from there to perceptions of her mother as not allowing her to cry for the lost father.

When I encouraged her to look at her own attempts to block access to her feelings about loss and vulnerability she exclaimed, in a tone of deep protest and anguish that:

If I really let myself feel the full love and hate that I *sense* I must feel, I don't think I could bear to feel *that real*! I'd feel human, and breakable....

As her voice tapered out, she let out a long sigh and remembered how puzzled and hurt she was when she broke off the relationship with her first boyfriend, whom she loved dearly. She had no idea why she had felt compelled to stop something that felt so right.

Maybe I just had to break his heart before he broke mine. But it felt like I broke something in myself as well: like my heart cracked....

But in the following months she seemed to disappear off the emotional radar screen altogether, hiding for sessions at a time under a "we can't really fix anything here, so why don't you admit it!", arms folded rigidly on the couch, type of resistance to looking at anything. Interpretations were met with a minimal grunt, followed by a yawned, sarcastic; "I suppose you might be right then...." Full stop. No elaboration. I persevered in linking this to the "Keep Out" sign in the lost city dream, and then one day (as I was at the peak of feeling rejected and unwanted) she started to cry and to apologize for treating me awfully. She had had a "change of heart" after seeing the preview of an episode in the rescue television series which she had scripted.

In this episode they had used a part of a song by the band Genesis, and this had set her crying uncontrollably. Luckily her partner was sitting next to her, and so it felt safe to cry. She remembered the words as:

Hold on my heart
just hold on to that feeling
we both know we've been here before
we both know what can happen
hold on my heart...
no matter where I go
she'll always be with me
so hold on my heart....

(I couldn't help but recall her reference in an early session to another song's:

"What's Love but a second-hand emotion?
Who needs a heart when a heart can be broken.")

Then she said: "I think I can bear the thought of losing you one day now. I couldn't before. But I'm not ready yet. I better work my guts out so I'll be ready."

The work did indeed intensify, and particularly so on two fronts, which seemed distinct, yet imperceptibly intertwined. One front concerned the business of sorting out just what sort of intimacy she could have with someone who was married or sexually unavailable, and yet whom she loved. Sorting out these Oedipal boundaries was very painful to her, but clarifications also produced consolations and a new freedom to be adventurous and playful once the boundaries were established. She found new ways of being intimate with both men and women which avoided the habitual problems of flirting destructively on the one hand, or denying herself possible intimacy too quickly, on the other.

The other front seemed to arise from her allowing her internal couple to be generative and for her internal mother to be repaired enough to be both fertile and imaginative in her feeding. It concerned the issue of regeneration/transformation—perhaps even metamorphosis, if we consider the reference to *Papillon*—as alternatives to depressing, claustrophobic stagnation inside the internal mother, with the dubious aim of controlling all intercourse as an "insider."

The first signs in the material of a struggle to take in what Bollas (1979) might call the transformational feeding mother, came at the end of a very frustrating session, when she half-jokingly, but triumphantly, asserted that food was a useless invention, because it was only ever transformed into stink. She seemed as surprised as I was to hear this outpouring from her infant self, and then admitted that she didn't know how to answer this. I reminded her that food is transformed into growth, and that only the leftover waste is stinky and excreted. Her whole tone changed, and she left the session as if smiling to herself. The following months were filled with death/decay versus transformation and regeneration battles. For example, a pair of plants on my veranda had supposedly died due to my neglect and failure to feed the right fertilizers or trace elements. In fact, all signs of life had disappeared in these pots, but I said to her that it was if she did not hold the possibility of regeneration or of seasons.

She agreed with this, but it was not until the following autumn, when the pots were filled with large, orange flowers, that she confessed that she had really thought at the time that I was just bluffing. (The doubting part of myself was also very relieved to see the evidence appear in the concrete form of the flowers.) This led to her taking a great interest in growing vegetables, and in particular she was fascinated by a new combination vegetable called brocci-flower, and by the ways in which plants produced new seeds. She read about exotic means by which seeds were digested by some animals and activated in the animal's gut, to be dispersed and germinated elsewhere. But most rewardingly for her, she discovered that she "was allowed" to be part of creation, transformation and regeneration.

Just before a termination date was set, she made a genuine discovery about herself and her relationships, which seemed to bring together the two "fronts" of analytical work. (That is, the Oedipal/separateness issues, and issues of a "faith" in life as transformational and regenerative.) The discovery was that she herself was capable of transforming her loved objects. For example, by offering love to her sometimes withdrawn partner, she saw that she could make him more loving and lovable. This discovery led to a new way of being in the world for her.

Previously, for example, she had seen a relationship as an acquisition, the success of which depended only on how successful she had been in winning the most "powerful, attractive" partner from a competition with other females. A kind of jungle lottery. To some degree this gave her enough faith to envisage a creative and loving life continuing and regenerating after her final session, although there was still much work to be done before termination, particularly on the cynical attack on this possibility. This manifested itself as a mocking sneering tone directed at those, including herself, who were willing to take responsibility for maintaining and protecting the fragile conditions within which life can exist, be enjoyed, and regenerate.

Discussion

I want to leave the clinical example here in order to say some more about the *omnipotent internal object* which I see as generating this mocking hatred of life, Love and Regeneration. In my view, the "seer" Tiresias in the Oedipus myth (not the level-headed Tiresias of Sophocles' *Antigone!*) illustrates the sort of internal "prophetic" object that I have in mind.

Grotstein (1980) alludes to a Magus/sorcerer figure who "casts spells on his victims and compels them to follow an enforced scenario from the Magus' life" (p. 368). I see Tiresias as having this effect on Oedipus (and, before him, Laius), and one way of understanding Oedipus' self-blinding is that it completes an identification with the blind Tiresias.

Tiresias had a huge Oedipal problem himself. According to Ovid (1986 edition), he once saw two giant snakes mating, struck at them, and was changed into a woman. Seven years later Tiresias again saw the two snakes and again attacked them, and was returned to manhood. Later, because of his double-sexed experience, he was called upon to settle a dispute between the gods Jove and Juno as to whether women or men get more enjoyment from sex. (Jove teased that women were better off, and Juno denied it.) Tiresias declared for women, and as a result was blinded by Juno. But Jove gave him a consolation in the ability to predict the future.

Internally, the Magus/Tiresian object says "No!" to the experiencing of the Oedipal feelings of longing, smallness, feeling left out of the parental relationship, and concern about one's murderous feelings towards them. The antidevelopmental consequence is that the emergence of the child's *whole* feelings towards the mother and father, including the true feelings about them preferring to mate with each other rather than with the child, is prevented. So then, the achieving of a spiritual/philosophical emotional perspective, where one can start to have feelings about these feelings, is impossible, if "Tiresias" rules the mind. In the depressive position, concerns about omnipotent, masturbatory wish-fulfillment are about the mocking and appropriating of the good object. In the spiritual position, the concern is that omniscient propaganda will block the experiencing of one's true feelings, and therefore the chance of having, at some point, a "philosophical" position about these feelings as they accumulate. Omnipotent, manic masturbatory states of mind not only attack the good internal object; they also prevent true feelings about feelings (ʃ) regarding life experiences; that is, Spirituality; because they replace the *experiencing* of life, and substitute for it what is *wished* for. And, therefore, one cannot develop and feel *Vergangenheitsbewältigung*, via the Inspirational Combining Object. Instead, one depends on the blindness of the Magus/Tiresian object who hates inspirational, combinatorial, musical mating to produce metamorphoses, and who therefore portrays it as a murderous, humiliating, incestual disaster which destroys insight, rather than producing the Shelleyan "light of love."

Tiresias—the voice of Omniscience—"says":

I've looked into/penetrated the insides of the Mother, from womb to guts, and can tell you that inside her is a father with a sharp weapon who wants to kill you; but if you kill *him* and get rid of him first, then the "lost city" inside her is all yours—so long as noone finds out what you've done—*and* Mother will go along with it all, because she really desires *you* most. And therefore nothing need change in your awareness of your place in the world, and your feelings about the world.

(Suttie [1935] believed that the child constructs the Oedipal myth as a

defense against feeling the pain of the Mother's rejection of the child as a
sexual partner. Apollinaire's [1918] surrealist farcical play, entitled "The
Breasts of Tiresias," also set as an opera by Poulenc, depicts the balloon-
breasts of the heroine Therese floating away on the breeze, revealing her to
be Tiresias the prophet, while her husband, by the power of thought alone,
brings into being no less than 40,049 babies.)

Note that the extra level of omniscient defensiveness that the *Tiresian*
object brings to that of the *"usual"* infantile omniscience is that the Tiresian
aim is to forestall (meaning "highway robbery") feelings about parental
coupling.

Seneca's *Oedipus* Tragedy is often regarded as inferior to Sophocles'
drama because it gives too much detail to the "blood-and-guts" methods by
which Tiresias divines Oedipus' past and future. But I tend to think that
Seneca was more "Kleinian" than Sophocles, and knew that the earliest
Oedipal turmoil was in relation to the fantasized inside of the mother's
body, including paranoid anxieties about how she might be combining with
the internal father and producing monstrous babies with him:

TIRESIAS:
    ... Had I youth and strength,
    I would receive the power of the god
    In my own person; we must find a way
    To probe Fate's secrets. (324-328)

TIRESIAS:
    Such evil portents in the sacrifice
    Are greatly to be feared. Tell me what signs
    You see in the entrails.

MANTO (His daughter):
    Father, what is this?
    ...The heart is shrunken,
    Withered, and hardly to be seen; the veins
    Are livid; part of the lungs is missing,
    The liver putrid, oozing with black gall.
    And here—always an omen boding ill
    For monarchy—two heads of swollen flesh
    In equal masses rise, each mass cut off
    And covered with a fine transparent membrane,
    As if refusing to conceal its secret.

On the ill-omened side the flesh is thick
And firm, with several veins, whose backward course
Is stopped by an obstruction in their way.
The natural order of the parts is changed,
The organs all awry and out of place.
On the right side there is no breathing lung
Alive with blood, no heart upon the left;
I find no folds of fat gently enclosing
The inner organs; womb and genitals
Are twisted and deformed. And what is this—
This hard protuberance in the belly? Monstrous!
A foetus in a virgin heifer's womb,
And out of place, a swelling in the body
Where none should be. It moves its limbs and whimpers
Twitching convulsively its feeble frame.
The flesh is blackened with the livid gore....
And now the grossly mutilated beasts
Are trying to move; a gaping trunk rears up
As if to attack the servers with its horns...
The entrails seem to run out of my hand.
That sound you hear is not the bellowing
Of cattle, not the cry of frightened beasts;
It is the fire that roars upon the altars,
The heart itself that quakes. (354-380)

Oedipus' eventual shame might also be his "Tiresian" rage and dismay at discovering that Laius was first and did have right of way.

The Emergence of a Feeling Philosophical Value System in the Spiritual Position

As the influence of the oracular omniscient internal object (Magus/ Tiresias) diminishes, a new leap forward seems to occur in the development of "whole object" relationships. I see this as beginning to occur at the time when the child is experiencing not just his or her separateness from each parent and their differences from each other, (working-through the depressive position), but is also beginning to realize and feel that his family is not the world. This is a very complex emotional realization, which is certainly a continuation of capacities developed as part of the working-through of the depressive position, and rests exclusively on these capacities.

But I think that at this level of development, a cognitive-emotional fusion occurs (perhaps Bion and Meltzer [1978] would say a holding together of loving, hating and wanting to know; L, H, and K) which produces a *feeling philosophical value system*—an emotional stance towards "the world." This would be a whole value system, in the sense of it having both a complete coherence and meaning to the person. It is deeply felt, or rather expresses the deepest feelings. The emotional coherence and wholeness would be developed over a lifetime, in the sense that this depends on sorting out, within oneself, what seems most important to one, and continuously developing ways of being in the world and of understanding the world according to orders of importance. The antidevelopmental alternative to this is to adopt a political manifesto or speech or cliché or fashionable doctrine, a pre-formed Group value system, and then see how many other people one can "convert," in order to prove its "Truth." An example of the type of whole feeling philosophical value system that I have in mind would be illustrated by Boethius' (1969 edition) *The Consolation of Philosophy.*

This is an ongoing dialogue which gradually evolves by deciding on the supremely important concern (in this case, a sense of "goodness") for the writer, and then reflecting on the relative values and meanings and implications for all other considerations in life, once the importance of a sense of goodness is fully accepted as always being the ultimate, meaningful aim. Meltzer (1978) sees such ordering of one's values as characterizing a "mature" personality which is motivated by aims, as compared with goals.

Perhaps the tension between the developing whole value system and the auto-sensual *part* value system is portrayed in the Golden Calf scene in the Old Testament. While Moses has travelled inward to receive his spiritual values in relation to living a life, the impatient group creates auto-erotic short term sensual gratification, and live day to day, promise to promise.

Again the evolution of God/Nature, internally, to beyond the parental, does certainly require the working-through of the depressive position—where the internal parents are given respect and freedom to be different—but it requires, even more dramatically, that distinctions be made between one's self and one's objects. At this stage, we know very little about this complex and mysterious achievement, although we do have common expressions like "she's her own person" or "he's his own man" to convey the display of it in personality.

(I have made a tentative attempt to explore the issue in another paper, [Maizels, 1995], on "Dis-Identification.")

The "Merlin-Father" in the Transformation of Schizoid Detachment into Observing-ego-in-feeling

Having said something about how the oracular-omniscient object substitutes predictive certainty and self-righteousness for the chance to step back from the canvas of one's life and get the "big picture" emotionally—to have an opportunity for *Vergangenheitsbewältigung*—a coming to terms with one's past and one's self, and to piece together what I have called a feeling philosophical value system—I now want to mention the internal object and process which might oppose such omniscience.

Put simply, I see the object which refuses the propaganda as linked to a whole-object version of the internal Father. I do not mean by this The Law of The Father, according to Lacan, which I see as a much more paranoid, thou-shalt-not-or-you'll-be-castrated if you do, construction of The Father in the child's mind. What I do mean lies somewhat beyond Meltzer's (1978) model of the development of the internal father, where the child unconsciously experiences him, at first, as possessing a weapon, and only much later in development experience him as having a "tool." In the painful, but potentially liberating emotional experience of getting a bigger perspective on the truth of one's feelings about life, the child needs, as it were, to be lifted onto the father's shoulders, in order to be able to face squarely the questions; "Well, how do you feel about all of this?" and "What seems important from up here, in this perspective?" And to feel that the father who once supported the containing mother, can now bear the weight of the child taking it's place in the tragi-comedy of life. From the case mentioned above, the dream of the "helicopter" function is most pertinent here. (In fact a recurring theme in the patient's scripts was of the importance of helicopters for getting people out of impossible places where they could not survive for very long.)

The father who provides this rescuing perspective might be called the Virgil father or perhaps the Yorick father, but because I think the process which I am describing here is well captured in the musical "Camelot" I will refer to him as the Merlin father, for argument's sake.

In "Camelot," poor old Arthur is distraught because Guinevere has paired with Lancelot, and seems not to be able to find a way of thinking about how he feels about the whole business. But he turns to Merlin, who tells him that he must become like an eagle, not to escape, but to get a wider emotional perspective on his feelings towards the couple and his values in life. This enables Arthur not to feel so persecuted, and to contain his murderous feelings, and to allow the boy in himself to have the freedom to live.

I see this Merlin-like capacity to get the eagle or helicopter view on one's feelings about life as harnessing previously schizoid tendencies of disengagement and emotional distance. In other words, through a trusting link with the internal father, the previously alienating role of the observer is now utilized in what I call the "observing-ego-in-feeling"—the capacity to see the broad canvas of one's emotional world, by standing back at some distance, and to have feelings about the canvas which can be thought about. This is not quite the same function as "the observing ego" in the Freudian sense, which has a much more intellectualized connotation, whereas the observing-ego-in-feeling has a more "artistic" connotation—in the sense that Art can be conceived of as showing one's feelings about life, or more accurately, one's feelings about all the feelings one has had in life. (Rhode, 1987, describes a patient who, in a moment of moving "musical" insight, "… had reached a turning point in his life: a moment, too, in which he could think to look over its entire span" [p. 118].)

The plangent quality of the observing-ego-in-feeling, its capacity to put music to one's emotional life, perhaps somewhat like the function of music in a film, gives to it a far more active role in the psyche than merely an organ for the perception of psychic qualities. It may streak a lightning flash of unexpected passion across a train journey, a walk in the park, or the perception of a stranger's face. When it swoops from its broader perspective it sucks in symbols and unifies themes in a maelstrom of meaning which can change a mind.

As Tennyson (1958 edition) versifies it in *The Eagle:*

> He clasps the crag with crooked hands;
> Close to the sun in lonely lands,
> Ringed with the azure world, he stands.
>
> The wrinkled sea beneath him crawls;
> He watches from his mountain walls,
> And like a thunderbolt he falls.

In Bion's language, alpha function is acting upon itself. (The snake of the One God eats up all the snakes of Pharaoh's conjurer.) It may be that the "limitation" of only being able to concentrate or focus on *one thing at a time* (consciously) is actually an "advantage" emotionally, because it foments a meta/transcendent, feelings about feelings state, and therefore becomes a path to "God/Oneness/The Infinite"—Bion's "O." The result is a transformation in "O"—one's ultimate reality, which can be avoided, ignored and perverted by the self. But if the self has faith in the transformation, that it will not be a catastrophe, but a generation of something new, then the self is transformed.

This will increase faith in the next transformation, made possible by the widened perspective of the observing-ego-in-feeling. In yet another language, the analyst is receptive to a wider perspective on the patient's emotional world firstly because he or she is (one hopes) less in the sphere of influence of the patient's defenses than the patient is, and secondly because of the augmentation of the perspective due to countertransference feelings. So the analyst may then "lift the patient" to that widened perspective and hold him or her there, as it were, on the analyst's shoulders, until the patient gets the wider perspective, *and* begins to introject the father whose shoulders are strong enough to hold him or her there.

In the depressive position, one pines for the lost good internal mother, and works it through by repairing her and then internalizing her. In the spiritual position, one pines for the father who allows the emotional experience and reaction to the loss—who says "How do you feel about not being able to possess mother's body and mind, and how does that help you to decide what's important for the rest of your life?" When the analyst has this transferential significance for the patient, above all others, then the analysis is ready for termination.

Here are two strikingly similar "examples," written almost 160 years apart, of a young man looking—perhaps for the first time—at the need for a coming to terms with his feelings about the World. Please note that both examples take place following cemetery scenes where the young men have just lost father figures.

The first is from Balzac's (1834) *Old Goriot* (*Father Goriot* in the original French).

> ... It was growing dusk, the damp twilight fretted his nerves; he gazed down into the grave, and the tears he shed were drawn from him by the sacred emotion, a single-hearted sorrow. When such tears fall on earth, their radiance reaches heaven. And with that tear that fell on old Goriot's grave, Eugene de Rastignac's youth ended. He folded his arms and gazed at the clouded sky; and Christophe, after a glance at him, turned and went—Rastignac was left alone.
>
> He went a few paces further, to the highest point of the cemetery, and looked out over Paris and the windings of the Seine; the lamps were beginning to shine on each side of the river. His eyes turned almost eagerly to the spaces between the column of the Place Vendôme and the cupola of the Invalides; there lay the great world that he had longed to penetrate. He glanced over that humming hive, seeming to draw a foretaste of its honey,

and said magniloquently: "We'll fight this out, you and I." (pp. 237-238)

The second example is from Paul Auster's (1989) *Moon Palace*.

I had come to the end of the world, and beyond it there was nothing but
air and waves, an emptiness that went clear to the shores of China. This is
where I start, I said to myself, this is where my life begins.
I stood on the beach for a long time, waiting for the last bits of sunlight to
vanish. Behind me, the town went about its business, making familiar late-
century American noises. As I looked down the curve of the coast, I saw the
lights of the houses being turned on, one by one. Then the moon came up
from behind the hills. It was a full moon, as round and yellow as a burning
stone. I kept my eyes on it as it rose into the night sky, not turning away
until it had found its place in the darkness. (pp. 306-307)

*Psychoanalytic and Artistic Technique. Sincere Post-Modernism versus Techno-
logical Juxtaposition*

Before concluding, I will briefly make two lines of suggestions, as
implications of the acceptance of a spiritual position in unconscious emotional life. The first concerns psychoanalytic technique and cannot easily, in
this discussion, be segregated from considerations of artistic technique. The
second line suggests a minimal revision of the theoretical terms previously,
often loosely, applied to the blanket term "depressive position," with the
hope of more precision. (I think that the reader will realize that these two
lines of suggestions are better seen as helical rather than parallel.)
Bion's (1970) technical suggestions—grounded in his models of container
-contained and the dreaming alpha-function enabled through maternal
reverie—give us an analytic object capable of holding, symbolizing and
modifying the infant's anxiety about dying, conveyed in its dread of
terrifying, fragmented and un-nameable persecutors. But Meltzer's (1973)
postdepressive combined object is more challenging than being "without
memory and desire." It is able to resonate deeply and trustingly with the
combined imaginativeness of the internal couple to produce not only the
occasional "inspiring" interpretation, but also the emotional ambience in
which this trust in the combined object's creativity may "work its magic."
Meltzer then links this level of unconscious mutual trusting with the
weaning process, and although he makes it clear that for this to happen
genuinely is a fairly rare business, it is nonetheless important as an indicator
of internal growth. (It also carries the risk of a mutually narcissistic mastur-

batory activity between patient and analyst.)

What I have to say about both analytic and artistic technique, particularly in relation to the "spiritual position" follows on from my thoughts about the transformation of the father inside the maternal container—from threat and rival, to the father who contains the mother's anxieties—in the infant's mind. The father in the mother must be able to bear the full force of the infant's feelings about being alive.

The "*Anti*" Magus-Tiresias analytic object interprets *both* the destructive phantasies towards the "combining" (Maizels, 1994) internal parents as well as the struggle to introject the inspiring ambience, or "music" of that creative, loving couple. This Merlin-like father in the maternal containing function, instills an emotional interest in the patient towards the *whole picture* of the patient's psyche. This requires a "stance" of the analytic object which fosters the spiritual position in the patient. Through appropriately "dual" transference interpretations, the patient can have feelings about the object which brings out the whole (subjective) truth of the patient's loving and hating phantasies.

Brenman-Pick (1995) describes an "even-handed" approach to the interpretation of both manic narcissistic trends in the patient as well as emphasizing the vulnerability, and Alvarez (1992) stresses the way that a patient's "wild lies" may also have a quality of potential space about them, into which a new self may be born. So the technique of the Merlin-like object would find a way of combining, with "musically-balanced" stresses of emphasis, both the regressive/resistive elements of the transference and the potentially progressive and imaginative. In this sense then, at the level of the "spiritual position," we might need a "kinder" re-evaluation of, for example, habits of the patient such as smoking or drinking. Where such habits may well have meant some sort of narcissistic fixation or intrusive identification for the patient at the level of paranoid-schizoid position, or denial of guilt at the level of depressive position, in the spiritual position they may well be functioning to give the patient a mental "cave" to "sigh" on feelings about life—feelings about all the emotional experience encountered so far.

In a sense, the analyst or therapist gives the "gift of time" by invoking such a spirituality in the patient, because it is (∫) which gives a sense of Time as it bundles good and bad experience together into a new perspective and gives one the sense of having "lived a life." (This work moves beyond the internalization of a repaired good object, as in the working-through of the depressive position, and yet all the emotional conflicts and defenses of the paranoid-schizoid and depressive positions will pertain towards the new "analytic object".)

There has been much controversy, especially in the past decade or so, about the value of the artistic "movement" known as "Post-Modern." If I apply my definition of "the spiritual position" to art, in the sense that art could be seen as a sincere attempt to convey one's feelings about a lifetime of feelings, then it becomes possible to tease out two strains of the post-modern ethos. One strain could be seen as an omnipotent attempt to appropriate all previous art as one's own—to possess it, by demonstrating nothing more than knowledge of its existence. The end result would be pastiche, or juxtaposition, with no emotional impact on the producer or the audience. At best we might hear a cultist, fashionable flurry of claims that it is "interesting."

The other strain would be experienced as conveying the artist's feelings about life by his or her "choosing" an idiosyncratic array of emotionally endowed "elements" and combining them in a way which produces a "universality," such that others will also be moved to experience their feelings about their lives.

Therefore, in both art proper, and in the artistic interpretation of transference phenomena, in the region of the spiritual position, the only important consideration with respect to "technique" is whether or not the analyst/artist is able to inspire a genuine "feelings about accumulated feelings" (ʃ) state in an-other. At this level of feeling (a meta level) the "tried and true" techniques can become a hindrance, especially if the "spirit" of the technique is lost sight of.

A Suggested Metapsychological Revision

The revision which I suggest here is not essential, since it covers aspects of emotional integration already intended by some who are satisfied with the term "depressive position." However, I now find it possible to be more precise, theoretically and technically, due to the aforementioned exploration of a "spiritual position," and of defenses against its achievements.

I suggest the term "reparative position" to replace the overinclusive term "working-through of the depressive position." This enables the term "depressive position" to keep its more literal meaning—that is, where love is depressed, and guilt is still experienced as largely persecutory, unhelpful and irreparable. In the "reparative position" then, one struggles to repair the good internal object, in the face of attacks upon its freedom as a whole separate entity.

I reserve the term "spiritual position" for an emotional capacity whereby one has further accepted the idea that all people lead separate, but potentially related lives, and that through a growing pattern of repeated feelings one sees one's own potential, responsibility and limitation for instigating transformations in oneself and others which bring about love and growth. In the spiritual position, one perceives that direct reparation of the internal objects is an omnipotent aim (Rhode, 1987; Meltzer, 1988). (Leontes can revive his love and good will towards Hermione—but it is not *he* who brings her "back to life.")

In the "reparative position" one attains a hope that one's love and concern can keep good objects in good repair. In the "spiritual position" one gains "heart" from a faith in regeneration-through-transfiguration, in spite of one's love and hate, and in spite of death. This process is only possible through *Vergangenheitsbewältigung*—an ongoing coming to terms with one's past through the "reverse barometer" of feelings about one's life, as one moves from pleasure principle to reality principle to psychic reality principle—from paranoid-schizoid to depressive to reparative. In this sense, the spiritual position is never really beyond the other positions; but more like a "steady lap" where one regains respite, hope, inspiration, faith or even dourness—at very least a sense of humanity through widened emotional perspective, before "plunging" back into the worlds of Ps - D - R. It's full ambience may grip us only occasionally, or even rarely, but its music rings in our souls each night as we clamber up and down Jacob's Ladder.

To recapitulate: the metapsychology of the spiritual position involves three interrelated elements of emotional growth.

1. The whole-object internalized father gives rise to an observing-ego-in-feeling which provides a "whole picture" perspective of one's emotional field.

2. The whole-object internalized mother gives a confidence in the re-generational, ever-transforming nature of the internal and external worlds.

3. The internalized creative combined object, which I have elsewhere called the "combining object" (Maizels, 1995), gives one a "heart" to bear the full force of feelings brought on by the whole-object mother and father.

In order to face death, one needs to accrue a heartening feeling that one's "life energy" has been transformed into a life. This feeling that one has lived a life—not just the knowledge that one has lived a life—is experienced through the three elements outlined above, which together comprise a "spiritual position."

Whereas the working-through of the depressive position (reparative position) enables the richness and poignancy of an "adagio" in the heart of the mind's music, in the spiritual position the self is heartened to feel this as yet only a "movement" in a whole symphony.

REFERENCES

Adamson, J. (1989). Hardy and idiosyncrasy–On individuality in Thomas Hardy's poems and tales. *Critical Rev.*, 29.

Alvarez, A. (1992). *Live Company: Psychoanalytic Psychotherapy with Autistic, Borderline, Deprived and Abused Children*. London: Tavistock/Routledge.

Auster, P. (1989). *Moon Palace*. London: Faber & Faber.

Balzac, H. (1834). *Old Goriot*. London: Penguin Classics, 1972.

Barrows, K. (1993). Book Review of *The Chamber of Maiden Thought*. *Int. J. Psycho-Anal.*, 74(1), 207-10.

Bion, W.R. (1970). *Attention and Interpretation*. London: Tavistock.

Boethius. (1969). *The Consolation of Philosophy*. London: Penguin Classics.

Bollas, C. (1979). The transformational object. *Int. J. Psycho-Anal.*, 60(1), 97-107.

Brenman-Pick, I. (1995). Concern: Spurious or real? *Int. J. Psycho-Anal.*, 76(2), 257-70.

Britton, R. (1989). The missing link: Parental sexuality in the Oedipus complex. In: J. Steiner (Ed.), *The Oedipus Complex Today*. London: Karnac Books.

Cummings, E.E. (1958). *95 Poems*. New York: Faber & Faber.

Dostoyevsky, F. (1871). *The Devils*. London: Penguin Classics, 1953.

Dickinson, E. (1993 edition). *New Poems of Emily Dickinson*. Chapel Hill: Harvard.

Fullerton, P. (1994). *The significance of the father for the sense of self*. Paper given to the Victorian Association of Psychotherapists, Melbourne.

Grinberg, L. (1978). The "razor's edge" in depression and mourning. *Int. J. Psycho-Anal.*, 59, 245-54.

Grotstein, J.S. (1993). Towards the concept of the Transcendent Position. *M. Klein Obj. Rel.*, 11(2).

—— (1980). Who is the dreamer who dreams the dream and who is the dreamer who understands the dream? In: J.S. Grotstein (Ed.), *Do I Dare Disturb the Universe? A Memorial to Wilfred Bion*. London: Maresfield.

Harris-Williams, M. & Waddell, M. (1991). *The Chamber of Maiden Thought*. London: Routledge.

Hinshelwood, R. (1989). *A Dictionary of Kleinian Thought*. London: Free Associations Books.

Ives, C.E. (1925). *114 Songs*. New York: Associated Music.

Jacques, E. (1965). Death and the mid-life crisis. *Int. J. Psycho-Anal.*, 46, 502-14.

Klein, M. (1961). *Narrative of a Child Analysis*. New York: Dell, 1977.

Maizels, N. (1994). Review article on *The Chamber of Maiden Thought*. M. *Klein Obj. Rel.*, 12(1), 93-103.

—— (1995). *Dis-identification*. Unpublished manuscript.

Meltzer, D. (1973). Routine and inspired interpretations: Their relation to the weaning process in analysis. Reprinted in: A. Hahn (Ed.), *Sincerity and Other Works*. London: Karnac Books. 1994, pp. 290-306.

—— (1978). *The Kleinian Development*. Perthshire: Clunie Press.

—— (1988) (with Harris-Williams, M.). *The Apprehension of Beauty*. Perthshire: Clunie Press.

Ovid (1986 edition). *Metamorphoses*. New York & London:Oxford University Press.

Rhode, E. (1987). *On Birth and Madness*. London: Duckworth.

Segal, H. (1964). *Introduction to the Work of Melanie Klein*. London: Hogarth Press.

Seneca (1966 edition). *Four Tragedies*. Middlesex: Penguin Classics.

Shelley, P.B. (1967 edition). Epipsychidion. In: *Complete Works*. New York & London: Oxford University Press.

Spillius, E. (1994). Melanie Klein's idea of the "total situation" in the transfer ence. Lecture given in Melbourne, Australia, August 25.

Suttie, I.D. (1935). *The Origins of Love and Hate*. London: Kegan Paul.

Tennyson, A. (1958 edition). *Collected Verse*. London: Abbey.

Waddell, M. (1986). Concepts of the inner world in the novels of George Eliot. *J. Child Psychother.*, 4(3).

Young, R. (1994). New ideas about the Oedipus complex. *M. Klein Obj. Rel.*, 12(2), 1-20.

ACKNOWLEDGEMENTS

Thanks to Antoinette Ryan for computorial and spelling help. Thanks to the readers from the *Journal of Melanie Klein and Object Relations* for valuable editorial advice. Thanks to Christine, for giving me the time which I ought to have given her.

38 Urquhart Street
Hawthorn 3122, Victoria
Australia

JOURNAL OF MELANIE KLEIN AND OBJECT RELATIONS
Vol. 14, No. 2, December 1996

CALL FOR PAPERS

The Journal of Melanie Klein & Object Relations cordially invites authors to submit papers for a Special Issue on:

MATTE-BLANCO

Contributors should send immediately a brief letter of interest, the title of their paper, and a summary of maximum 250 words. Send manuscripts to the Editor by *September 1, 1997*. All manuscripts should conform to the style of this publication (see "Instructions to Authors").

* * *

CALL FOR COLLABORATION

For a volume tentatively titled

W.R. BION: AN INTERNATIONAL ANNOTATED BIBLIOGRAPHY

we need listings and brief summaries/descriptions of books, articles, studies, letters, photographs, recordings by and about the late Dr. Wilfred R. Bion. Authors fluent in German and Spanish are especially needed. Each author will be listed under the contributed entry. Mail or fax immediately letter of interest and inquiries to:

esf Publishers
Bion Biblio Project
1 Marine Midland Plaza
East Tower-Fourth Floor
Binghamton, New York 13901, USA.
Fax: (607) 723-1401

A PSYCHOANALYTIC APPROACH TO ADDICTION: THE FORMATION AND USE OF A PRECOCIOUS PARANOID-SCHIZOID-DEPRESSIVE ORGANIZATION

Enid B. Young

Historically, psychoanalysts have not considered people with addictions as appropriate for analysis. With the exception of a small number of analysts in England (Meltzer, 1973), France (Anzieu, 1989, 1990; McDougall, 1989; Rey, 1994), Argentina (D. Rosenfeld, 1991), and this country (Krystal, 1970), the treatment of addictions has been confined to psychotherapists and the self-help community, most notably, twelve-step programs. However, addictions such as eating disorders, alcoholism, sexual addiction, and workaholism, have been increasingly noted in borderline, narcissistic, and schizoid patients. These patients are often highly competent, intelligent, and accomplished people. Yet, addictions cause suffering in their lives, and are often a hidden impediment in the therapeutic process. In the past, I have written about the connection between the development of addictions and the occurrence of early traumatic experiences, such as incest (Young, 1991). As I continued to question the prevalence of addictions in my patients, I observed the presence of certain anxieties that led me to believe that the etiology of addiction can be traced to even earlier traumatic occurrences. This paper will address the theoretical and practical implications of this observation.

Clinical Phenomena that Illuminate the Etiology of Addiction

A recurrent experience in the analytic setting helped me to understand the nature of my patients' anxieties. Material presented frequently suggested a paranoid-schizoid mode of relating, as defined by Melanie Klein (1975). However, my patients were not amenable to such interpretations. Furthermore, this material elicited strong physical sensations in me, such as tightness, shortness of breath, confusion, an hypnotic-like apathy, or extreme frustration. The intense and concrete quality of these sensations suggested more primitive modes of communication than projective identification. The experience of being bombarded, and the way these sensations "clung" to me, even when the patient was not present, corresponded more with intrusive and adhesive identification, as described by Meltzer et al. (1975), Tustin (1981), and Bick (1967).

Wondering about the primitive quality of my patients' communications, I turned to psychoanalytic theories of very early, elemental forms of development such as those of Bion, Anzieu, Tustin, Bick, Winnicott, and Gaddini. I began to understand that my patients' behavior indicating a paranoid-schizoid mode was actually something different. I concluded that these manifestations were, in fact, a pseudo paranoid-schizoid mode that served as a protective covering, like the hard shell of a tortoise, protecting a wounded and defective surface, analogous to what Esther Bick (1967) calls a "second-skin" (p. 115).

My patients seemed to fear fragmentation due to a lack of a well-constituted boundary, that is, in an intermediate area between psyche and soma. Without this boundary, they feared that the fragile self could not hold its shape. For example, one patient spoke about my words coming at her like sharp knives, piercing her. Another patient managed her fear of fragmentation by imagining what I was going to think about various aspects of her behavior, and then confusing her imagined me with what had actually happened. I could exist for her only as her own creation. Another patient spoke of feeling torn apart, and "decimated" when I would point out particular features of her behavior.

It appeared to me, then, that the paranoid-schizoid like mode of behavior was a barrier the patient placed between us to protect his or her fragile surface. The violent reactions that sometimes occurred in response to my interpretations related to the surface, as if wounds had been touched. What I took as a "paranoid" position was exacerbated. When I did not interpret in that manner, but remained largely silent—that is, thinking, feeling and speculating to myself—a quieting down ensued, as if an integration were occurring right before me. I will give an example to illustrate my observation.

A thirty-three-year old male doctor entered psychoanalysis with complaints about a lack of intimacy with his partner, and a disquiet with his life in general. An alcoholic who had not been drinking for two years, he was also concerned about his obesity, which had been a difficulty since childhood. In initial stages of the analysis, he presented material of a paranoid nature. He complained about people treating him badly, cheating him, and generally abusing him. My attempts to interpret his own behavior brought me into the realm of those who were abusing him, and he would respond in an angry and derogatory manner. My experience with him in the room was one of fear. I found myself feeling very anxious, and timid about responding to him. He also talked about experiencing my words as daggers that were penetrating him, or rocks being hurled at him. I correspondingly experienced a feeling that his surface was so badly bruised that any sound coming from me was likely to wound him. A few months into the analysis, he told me that he felt he needed silence from me. I thought to myself that this request was an attempt to control me, but at the same time, I felt that he was correct, that he did need silence. I said nothing for several weeks. I continued to feel anxiety, in particular on the weekend breaks. I found, however, that gradually my feelings of anxiety began to lift, and correspondingly his productions became more cohesive. He was better able to think, and I began to offer brief interpretations that he was able to use. One day he said to me, "I notice that I can listen to your words now in a way I couldn't before. I'm wondering how that happened." Later on he described the change, saying, "I don't feel like I'm spilling out through the holes in my self anymore. I feel self-contained, and it's such a pleasure."

I wondered about the relationship between my observations and the pervasive presence of addictions in my patients. In turning to psychoanalytic theorists who have delineated major ongoing failures in the earliest experiences of the mother-infant dyad, in particular Frances Tustin's work on autism (1981), I arrived at a new understanding of addiction. I hypothesized that the pseudo paranoid-schizoid material described above indicated a precocious, or prematurely formulated, paranoid-schizoid-depressive position, and that addictions play a role in maintaining this organization. This theory of addiction, which I believe involves disturbances in the containment relationship of the mother-infant dyad, suggests a new tack for the treatment of addiction in the analytic setting.

The Nature of the Developmental Problem in the Etiology of Addiction

Melanie Klein posited inherited psychological capacities that unfold in normal maturation. Klein's depiction of the process of integration, or the movement toward wholeness in self and object, begins with the vicissitudes of the paranoid-schizoid and depressive positions.

Klein's use of the word "position" to emphasize the dynamic relationship between the paranoid-schizoid and depressive positions was elaborated by Bion (1984). Bion suggested that the two positions were in a "chemical" equilibrium with each other, that is, a constantly fluctuating interrelationship. In this presentation, I concur with Bion's conception of the inseparability of the two positions.

Several theorists hypothesize that anxieties, or integrative tasks, exist prior to the consolidation of the Kleinian paranoid-schizoid and depressive positions. Grotstein (1994) notes that the work of Meltzer, Bick, Marcelli, Tustin, Bion, and Ogden, as well as himself in his conception of the black hole experience (1991), posits a position, or anxieties, more primitive than Klein's positions. Grotstein also argues for the simultaneity of these positions (1994). One might say, then, that certain anxieties may be foremost at specific developmental junctures.

For Winnicott (1958), normal development is predicated on the assumption that a primary state of unintegration exists, which should lead, without interference of a traumatic nature, and with adequate provisions from the environment, toward an ever-evolving state of integration. Similarly, Gaddini (1992) suggested that integrative processes are the first function of self-organization.

In elaborating Klein's notion of projective identification, Bion also described early integrative tasks. Bion (1962) posited a container-contained relationship between subject and object, asserting that this relationship is essential to the creation of an internal space and the subsequent development of symbolic processes. Bion stated that the function of the mother is to transform the unassimilated sensations of the infant's experience through her capacity to assimilate (understand) the child's projections and return them to the child in a metabolized form. Also in this tradition, Anzieu (1990) and Bick (1967) postulate that the initial task in the state of unintegration is the creation of a sense of a boundary within which an internal and external reality can be distinguished and, ultimately, the tasks of individuation accomplished. Anzieu called this boundary the skin ego, following Freud's statement that the ego is "first and foremost a bodily ego; it is not merely a surface entity, but is itself the projection of a surface (1923)."[1]

Anzieu stated that the skin ego is an intermediate structure between the mother and the infant and the inner psychic world and the exterior world. The skin of the ego forms the boundary of the ego, or holds the ego together, and thereby determines the integrity or cohesiveness of the ego. Anzieu asserted that the skin ego is inscribed in potential form on the psyche at birth, and that if the appropriate experiences do not occur at the correct moment, the structure is not acquired, or is distorted.

Esther Bick, greatly influenced by Bion, made discoveries that corresponded closely with Anzieu's formulations, though neither originally knew of each other's work. She stated that the primitive parts of the personality are felt to have no binding force and must therefore be held together by the skin functioning as a boundary. Bick specified that the formation of a cohesive skin boundary depends upon the successful containment of the infant by the mother. In her seminal article, "The Experience of the Skin in Early Object Relations", Bick (1967) asserted that an experience of being contained by the maternal function evolves into a sense of having a container, which mitigates the terror of separation from the mother by becoming itself the source of containment.

Bick also asserted that disturbance in the primal skin function can lead to the development of a "second-skin" formation. Dependence on the object is replaced by a pseudo-independence or by the inappropriate use of certain mental functions for the purpose of creating a substitute for this skin container function.

These theories all imply that the task of the creation of an internal space takes place prior to the consolidation of the paranoid-schizoid and depressive positions.

Frances Tustin's (1981) work on autism provides a further conceptual tool for understanding pathology that arises when traumatic events occur in the state of unintegration. She described autism—distinguished from a pathology based on constitutional factors—as psychological functioning which has been halted by awareness of too-early bodily separation from the nursing mother. This traumatic separation occurs at a time when the infant does not distinguish the mother's body from its own. Internal structures are thus not sufficiently organized to stand the strain of separation. The infant turns away from live human contact and uses autistic objects (metal toys) and autistic shapes (head-banging, rocking, wall-kicking) to create a protective armor that denies separateness. The use of these mechanisms precludes integration.[2]

A Psychoanalytic Theory of Addiction: Premature Development

In describing disruptions in early integrative processes, several theorists (Greenacre [1953], Gaddini [1992], Winnicott [1958;1965], James [1960], Bick [1967]) have drawn attention to the consequences of premature development. This is a kind of "forced growth" in which precocious gains are made at the expense of a consolidated self.

I would like to suggest that, contrary to commonly held beliefs, the main issue with regard to addiction is not regression or states of collapse, but the consequences of such precocious growth. This theory of the etiology of addiction, then, contributes

182   YOUNG

significantly to our understanding of the pathology of premature development.

It is in the movement from unintegration to integration that I believe the etiology of addiction occurs. I am proposing that an essential aspect of the suffering in addiction may relate to inadequacies in the containment relationship of the mother-infant dyad. This leads to the faulty development of the psychological boundary or skin ego. The distorted development of a second or substitute skin will take place to compensate for the inadequate skin ego. Normal psychological processes of integration will be interrupted.

In Kleinian theory, the earliest forms of object relatedness in the paranoid-schizoid and depressive positions entail specific gains in both structure and function. I believe that when infants have not achieved a secure skin ego, this consolidation cannot be achieved. Instead, the infant will use his or her inherent mental equipment to grab on to whatever can be used from the paranoid-schizoid and depressive positions. This results in premature development, and the formation of a distorted paranoid-schizoid-depressive position.

Addiction becomes an external organizing force in this second-skin container, which ultimately assumes its own physiological, psychological, and social autonomy. I want to suggest an analogy here. Addictions function within the precocious organization in the same way that autistic objects and shapes do in the auto-sensuous world of the autistic child. Tustin believes that infants use autistic objects and shapes to prevent the awareness of separation. Similarly, addictions maintain an illusion of separateness; they actually function to deny and to prevent psychological separation. She points out that the fixation to autistic mechanisms as a means of feeling held together denies the reality of human contact and thereby leads to deterioration. Addictions also provide a sense of being held together that denies and prevents authentic relationship, leading to both psychological and actual death.

Addictions may be said to be a symptom of a deficiency in the perimeter of the self. Because the perimeter is not secure enough, the individual cannot distinguish between inside and outside, or where self and other begin and end. The infant's premature use of the still inchoate internal mechanisms of the paranoid-schizoid-depressive positions protects the fragility of the skin-ego and replaces reliance on the maternal function. Addictions then function to ward off catastrophic awareness of actual separation that cannot be sustained because of the lack of a cohesive skin-ego.

For example, whereas addictions create an illusion of dependence, whether to a substance or a person, they actually function to deny authentic dependence. What looks like dependence is, in fact, an adhesive or intrusive dynamic, like algae or barnacles sticking to a rock. This is vividly portrayed in the case of a twenty-six-year-old female patient who entered therapy in a crisis regarding a relationship at work. She felt strongly attached to a male co-worker and had felt cruelly rejected by him. She seemed to be describing a lengthy and deep attachment. In fact, she had dated this man only once. The day following the date she had felt slighted by him, and began writing notes to him in which she chastised him for his abandonment and betrayal of her. She was obsessed with him and unable to eat or sleep. She also revealed that she had enacted this pattern repeatedly with many men. We eventually understood that her fixations provided a protective cover for her, a whirling dark cesspool that tormented her and yet protected her fragile boundary by preventing any authentic contact, which she believed would destroy her.

This precocious development does allow, to a certain extent, for achievements and often the semblance of a "normal" or "relational" life. But in fact, human contact has been distorted, and separatedness[3] within the dyadic relationship has not occurred. Until addictions are given up, the development of the self is impeded. Integration cannot proceed, and the normal paranoid-schizoid and depressive positions cannot evolve.

The Contribution of Pathological Containment to the Formation of Addiction

On the basis of clinical observation, I think it is possible to delineate a specific problem in the infant/mother dyad that is germane to the etiology of addiction.

When the maternal container itself has not been well-formulated, the maternal object may unwittingly use the infant for the purposes of alleviating the defects in her own skin ego.

What I am emphasizing here is not only the incapacity of the maternal object to receive the infant's raw sensations, but specifically the placement of the maternal object's own anxieties into the infant for the purposes of containment.

The infant, not having the means to form a container, is enabled to feel held together by serving this function for the mother. The infant develops the omnipotent fantasy of being the parent to the parent. Psychologically, the infant lives inside the mother's skin ego and believes that they thus keep each other alive. The two are arrested in time and are confined to a single space. This belief then becomes the core of the primary dread— separation equals death. As one patient put it:

Why did I take in my mother? To go right into me like water. Through my skin. I think of being in the womb and then being born. She doesn't realize that I'm born. She treats me as if I'm still inside her. I feel I don't exist. I feel I'm still inside her. An unborn child. I needed her to do it because I couldn't do it. To be there and then be ready to let go. That process of separation.

When there has been adequate maternal containment, one might say that the mother lives initially in the sensations related to the skin and gradually is taken in as a good internal object. The central organizing metaphor is "leaning back" into the belly of the maternal object, as described by Anzieu (1989), and articulated by Grotstein (1991) in a background presence of primary identification.

When failure in the containment relationship leads to premature development, relatedness is feared and repudiated. Instead of leaning back, there is a maintenance of rigidity. The failure to internalize a cohesive container results in the lack of a reliable surface to lean back against, which could support integration. Neither normal dependence nor authentic independence develops.

Addiction creates an illusion of relatedness. Addictive behaviors do not substitute for the maternal object, but rather deny that the maternal object is separate and needed for creation and sustenance.

Rather than describing addiction as a deficiency in self-regulation, it is more exact to say that addiction is a manifestation of regulation by an omnipotent, defective self which is terrified of and thereby opposed to human relationships.

The consequence for the infant in usurping the parental role is a pervasive sense of inadequacy, illegitimacy, and persecution. The result of not being contained appropriately is that the infant feels "uncontainable."

Case Study

In this vignette, I would like to show several points: (1) how the analysand both communicates and seeks to protect the fragility of the skin ego through the precocious paranoid-schizoid-depressive position; (2) the strong interconnection between the analyst and the analysand as the patient sheds the second-skin layer and forms an authentic "alive" skin; (3) the requirement of sensitivity and at the same time, discipline, and nonparticipation in the pathological organization, that is required of the analyst; and (4) the role of addictions in the pathological organization.

Mr. M. is a 38-year-old Caucasian male. He has never been married, and lives alone in a home that he owns. He has been an employee of a large company for many years, is respected for his work, and given frequent promotions.

Mr. M. entered psychoanalysis four times a week because of an inability to form intimate relationships. He explained that he considered himself a "sex and love addict." He either engaged in sexual relationships that held no intimacy but that he became very attached to, or avoided sexuality altogether for long periods of time. He also complained of a food addiction, which he described as compulsive eating of sugar-laden foods such as ice cream, followed by strict dieting because of a fear of obesity. He had attended 12-step program meetings and occasionally continued to do so.

I am going to report a period of time that I believe reveals the nature of Mr. M.'s anxieties with regard to his skin ego.

Mr. M.'s presentation throughout the first two years of the analysis was characterized by a hypnotic-like droning. Pseudo-intellectualization substituted for thinking. It was as if he were addicted to his own mind, fascinating himself with his words. In this way he used words to control himself and the analyst. Mr. M.'s fear of taking in manifested in his inability to use words to think and make meaning, and his refusal to take in my words.

Interpretations directed toward this behavior were reacted to with anger. He would accuse me of demeaning and dismissing him. Or even worse, he would sometimes agree with my interpretations and continue on in the same manner, with this issue now as the content of his ruminations.

I felt a palpable frustration. The sense that he was a caricature of himself, a role rather than a human being, was quite strong. I felt as if I were up against an impenetrable barrier that, from whichever direction I approached, would reassert itself.

I surmised, from the feelings of despair and lack of control that I felt, that his fear of being out of control was of traumatic proportions—in Bion's terms, a "nameless dread." I felt that while I needed to be present with him, despite his attempts to eliminate my existence, I also needed to find a way to let him discover the control for himself. I thought that this was the crucial factor in a containment experience for him at this point.

When I was silent during one hour, he became anxious. He said he felt I was being critical of him by not responding. I felt his tension and my own need to alleviate his tension—but remained quiet and curious. He was then able to reveal that when he spoke, he was preoccupied with what my response would be to his productions. He saw that he attempted to fascinate me with his analytic chatter and experience us both as being under his control. In this way he eliminated the possibility of any spontaneous feelings of aliveness that might emanate from himself or from me. I felt an opening in his protective cover as he spoke, and a feeling of connection with him as a person that had been missing.

A few sessions later, he became angry with me for the first time in an authentic and alive way. However, in the next hour, when I referred to the aliveness of the previous hour, he denied expressing anger. He took the position that I had persecuted him, and that he had accepted it passively. Relationships were, as he knew all along, impossible. I was very puzzled.

Over the next few weeks, I gently but persistently wondered out loud about his denial of his authentic anger. Gradually, my wondering became his wondering with me, and he was able to tell me that it was both a defeat and a threat for him to have related to me in an alive manner. He saw that it was the control part of him, his protective, impenetrable covering, that was threatened. He began to see how pervasive this covering was. He said, "I can't bear the feelings, so I'm going off into my mind. As soon as I notice that I am alive, I have to run for cover again. My mind wants to rush in—it's the control thing—like darting out and looking for all the dangers. Just now, thinking about what's going on for me, I can't deal with it anymore. This control part of me. It gets so convoluted. If it gets to where the control is in danger, it will begin to do loops in my mind or shut me down." I experienced him as more alive at this time, as if he had shed another layer of his second skin. And I felt an aliveness in myself that I had not previously experienced with him.

He revealed new information about his relationship to food. He told me that he felt panic at the thought of being hungry. So that he would make sure he had food with him wherever he went. At the same time, he was extremely fearful of what he put into his body. He would alternate between an obsessive attitude about what he ate and sugar binges. We were able to understand that taking in was tantamount to destruction because of the fragility of his surface. He was therefore never able to be satisfactorily filled, and endured a state of emotional starvation in order to control the possibility of anything going into him. He then attempted to ameliorate the starvation with binging, and then to get rid of the poisonous contents by strict dieting. His sexual addiction followed the same pattern.

I believe that Mr. M. has had to compensate for a skin ego so fragile and absorbent that he could not rely upon it to enable him to give or receive without danger. Aliveness was intensely feared because of the threat that it would tear him apart, or, in his words, "draw him into a black hole of insanity." His rigid crust-like covering allowed him to traverse increasingly complex levels of development without being destroyed.

The development of a second skin served the purpose of compensating for his lack of a well-constituted boundary, as well as compensating for his mother's defective skin ego. This is what Henri Rey (1994) calls "omnipotent reparation." Omnipotent reparation, because it can never be realized, creates rigidity and stagnation, rather than the growth that evolves from depressive position reparation. The patient, then, as Rey points out, brings his mother to the analyst to be repaired, as well as himself.

I feel that difficulties in acknowledging the presence of the analyst in the first year of the analysis in particular, were related to difficulties in allowing himself to emerge from his fused connection with his mother's skin-ego, and to relinquish the reversal of roles by acknowledging dependence on the analyst. Such an emergence posed a threat to himself, as well as to his fantasized mother. The danger was also to me, because he did not believe that my skin ego could contain him, as his mother's did not. He believed that he would cause my destruction, as he believed that he was the cause of his mother's incapacities.

As he has begun to internalize a cohesive container, he has increasingly developed a sense of having an inner life, experiencing himself and the analyst as having an inside and an outside. Thus, both he and the analyst have begun to "take shape" for him as real, alive, and separate identities.

The Addicted Self

Addictions maintain a fragile self that is continually undermined by the lack of a cohesive skin ego. I believe that the addicted self attempts to maintain itself in this condition in the following ways.

The addicted self is frozen in a state of terror because its borders are inadequate. Experience is on a concrete, physical, two-dimensional surface. Symbolic processes are curtailed. The development of internalized relationships is also curtailed because of a preoccupation with the surface.

Addicted people use paranoid-schizoid-depressive mechanisms to prevent relating, rather than to facilitate relating, with all of its vicissitudes. Covert alliances substitute for dynamic human relationships. "Dramas" related to feelings of persecution, retaliation for mistreatment, and self-recrimination, characterize interactions. Depressive anxieties as defined by Klein do not exist, because the destruction of "relating" to the object has not been acknowledged. Only when truly relating can the object then be destroyed and repaired—that is, loved and hated. Instead, as I have shown with Mr. M., omnipotent reparation predominates—for example, in the fantasy of keeping the mother alive through the fusion of skins.

Projective identification does not develop into a mechanism for the formation of an internal world of thinking and feeling. Instead, adhesive and intrusive identification predominate, as described by Meltzer and Bick.

That is, as I have shown with my twenty-six-year-old female patient, the addicted self projects on to the surface of the object, and thereby fantasizes being stuck to the object (adhesive identification). Or, projections are used to invade and possess the object (intrusive identification), leading to a fantasy of ownership, as well as entrapment (claustrophobia). Splitting, idealization, projection, introjection, reparation, and identification, normally used to establish differentiation, are used to maintain the fantasy of fusion. But the price of fusion is the twin terror of engulfment and abandonment.

Psychological life for the addict is dominated by an acute sensitivity on the surface which results in a constant oscillation between "pleasant" and "unpleasant" sensations and fluctuating impulses to "attach" and to "sever," to "entrap" and to "escape." The distortions in the skin ego as the limiting membrane result in fantasies, dream-life, and relationships suffused with fears of being trapped, suffocated, cooked alive, tortured, penetrated. A feeling of "wrongness" permeates and substitutes for conscience. On the other hand, the omnipotent fantasy of keeping the mother alive creates an illusion of self-esteem.

Differentiation between the genders and between body parts tends to be blurred. The breast, penis, and anus are equated and the sensations belonging to each zone are not differentiated. *One might say that the mother is in everything*—so that sexuality is defined predominantly by the sensations (longings, needs) related to the dyadic relationship. The addictive quality of so-called sexual relationships thus ensues.

As I described in the case of Mr. M., the use of the mind to control mimics the use of the mind for thinking. This often takes the form of obsessive ruminating or hysterical dramatization. This condition is described by Winnicott (1965) as the overuse of the mind, or the mind usurping the environment function, leading to a disconnection between psyche and soma. The mind is not located in the body. In the analytic setting, free association is feared, because the mind is used to control rather than to inquire. Spontaneous or "new" thoughts (in Bion's terms, linking) are avoided. Thoughts may be said to "skim on the surface" and are used to provoke reactions, or more specifically provide sensations, which substitute for relatedness.

The development of emotions is arrested. Rather, sensations and random affects, colored mainly by a diffuse anxiety, abound. Emotions are experienced as material—as objects to be used, avoided, manipulated, and as concrete sensations which threaten the fragile and defective boundary formation. For example, excitement cannot be contained because it would shatter the entire system. Anger is a relentless, impinging, gripping, and explosive sensation that torments the mind and can only be released through destructiveness or exhaustion. Anxiety substitutes for aliveness. What is defended against is the terror of "limitless diffusion."

The potential for the mature expression of love and aggression does not evolve. Instead, a sense of persecution prevails, generating an oscillation between passivity and violence. Love is a never ending drama of being used or using. Love is taken for an erotic sensation, upon which the cohesiveness or destruction of the skin ego boundary depends. Aggression takes the form of manipulation of the other to control the dangers inherent in the environment. Authentic love and aggression are feared because they imply a differentiated self, which would sever the shared skin between the child and the maternal object—as seen so clearly in Mr. M.'s adamant denial of his emerging authentic anger.

The addictive behaviors which characterize this organization become a disease in itself, increasingly taking over all functioning. Following its own laws, without intervention this disease leads to the final extinction of the possibilities inherent in the incipient self. What is set in motion is a disintegration process rather than an integration process.

Discussion

Gabbard (1991) notes that numerous authors (Boyer, Giovacchini, Grotstein, Little, Searles) have focused on the centrality of containment in the treatment of the borderline patient. He asserts that it would be erroneous to view containment as inferior to interpretation in terms of its therapeutic potential. He specifies several active aspects of the containment process, such as silent processing, verbal clarifications of what is going on inside the patient and in the patient-analyst dyad, an ongoing self-analytic process to delineate the analyst's own contributions to the struggles with the patient, and the silent interpretation of what is going on inside the patient in preparation for later verbal interpretation.

When a patient presents initially with a precocious paranoid-schizoid-depressive organization, it is an indication of the analysand's acute distress with regard to the deficiencies in his or her ability to contain and preserve psychological existence. If the distress is "received" by the analyst through a process of containment, rather than "reacted to" with interpretations directed to the content of the material, the analysand will feel hopeful about being welcomed for his or her own individual existence, a possibility that was thwarted by the original failure in containment.

I am suggesting that the first task of the patient and the analyst in the analytic setting is to address the damaged container of the patient. It is the body-ego which is being formulated, so that the process might be described as a psycho-biological development. The analyst must be present to a relationship with the analysand in which the analyst can be used even more primitively than on the level of part-object usage. This process will eventually lead to the diffusion of the skins of the subject and maternal object, and the creation of a cohesive inner space within which a normal paranoid-schizoid-depressive constellation can evolve.

The analyst is not, in the beginning, an object to be internalized. He or she is a threat to be manipulated through engagement in complex dramas. There is no interior space within which to internalize, or, rather, there is a corrupted interior space. Therefore, for the analysand, as I mentioned with regard to the fear of fragmentation, there can be only one person in the room to begin with. The initial task in the analytic setting is the creation of a secure skin or boundary of the ego, so that the creation of a cohesive interior can take place, and two people can emerge in the analytic setting.

A strict analytic frame is crucial because the original pathological adjustment is made with regard to boundaries. Pushing the analytic frame, enlisting the analyst as an advice-giver and enlisting the analyst as a persecutor are some of the many complex ways that the patient will attempt to engage the analyst. Analysts will often interpret in the paranoid-schizoid mode, when in fact such maneuvers are attempts to maintain the second skin of the pathological organization. Without a clear analytic frame and a conscientious analytic stance, engagement with the analysand in pathological fusion will inevitably result. The emergence of appropriate dependence will be precluded. Effective analytic treatment depends upon an appropriate process of containment, which necessitates a framework without interference.

Initially, I believe that the crucial feature of the analytic interaction is pre-symbolic. The "felt" experience of the analyst takes center stage. Because the analysand communicates through eliciting sensations, the analyst will be flooded with strong sensory experiences. As previously described, emotions and physical sensations will often "stick to" or "intrude into" the analyst, creating an inability to think or understand. The analyst's own second-skin mechanisms may be evoked to ward off the discomforting sensations.

Many analysts, such as Joseph (1989), Ogden (1989), Grinberg (1990), and Gabbard (1991), have discussed how difficult it is for the analyst to withstand the strong sensory input. An awareness of the disintegrating self helps the analyst to understand that such communication by the analysand indicates the presence of the precocious paranoid-schizoid-depressive organization, and thereby to work on the level of containment.

In this territory, such factors as the rhythm of the analyst's interventions and silence, and tone of voice in particular, are highly significant. The analysand experiences the analyst's attention itself as concrete. The analysand is "held" by the analyst's attention or "dropped." The quality of attention (countertransference) to the analysand's state in the moment is decisive with regard to the formulation of interpretations that are tolerable to the analysand. The initial phase of the analytic process is often marked by discomfort, as mistakes are made and corrected (analogous to the process described by Winnicott between mother and infant), until a therapeutic alliance or "rhythm of relating" is established.

Because the patient lives on a defective (wounded) surface, all interventions—words or silence—are likely to be experienced concretely. Thus, patients often describe that the words of the analyst come at them like blows, or daggers. Words may be experienced as concrete entities that "fall" on a sensitized surface. Depending on the specific nature of the surface, they may, for example, bounce off, penetrate, fall through holes and intrude, or fuse into a spongy surface and not be heard. Understanding and misunderstanding by the analyst are likewise often experienced as concrete physical sensations of "soothing" or "wounding." One patient described this experience by saying:

I know I hurried past what you said, ignoring it. I think that's what happened. But as I thought about it, there's something else there too. It's another example of a comment coming in and penetrating me. I can't keep it out and think about it. So the only way I could deal with it was to ignore it. I'm not sure how to describe it better. If I can't protect myself—what is the boundary of the self? Why can't I be self-contained? You make a simple comment, you're observing. Still, it's like a spear that penetrates, that lodges in my brain. I don't know why. It makes me feel very sad.

If the manifestations of the pathological organization are interpreted directly before a "good-enough" container has been established, the patient may feel criticized and attacked. Such interpretations may be experienced as a kind of "skinning," a pulling off of the second skin that is felt as a shameful, painful exposure. Because misunderstanding leads to a sense of being "skinned," and thereby rejection and despair, there may be rage and retaliation. *Gradually, as a sense of being contained leads to the availability of a container, the container will serve as an authentic skin within which the analysand can reflect, and be subjective, rather than fused with the object.*

Many analysts mistakenly take the extreme reaction of such patients as an overly punishing superego reaction. In fact, I believe that a cohesive superego has not been formed, but is distorted by the deficiencies in the skin ego. The sense of being wrong is not related to guilt, but to the necessity of maintaining the second-skin, and is often evoked when interpretations assume a symbolic process that is not possible. Premature interpretations reactivate the initial trauma and sense of rejection.

This pathological organization has affected all developmental sequences and therefore each stage of development must be found anew in the analytic setting. The disintegrative state will be returned to continuously as the analysand experiences the terror related to integration.

As the second skin is relinquished, the patient finds the analyst on the level of need. The experience of being held becomes predominant. The concern is not yet on the level of sexuality; it is, rather, on the level of holding and handling. *The need that is being addressed is a skin that can be touched.* This process allows the analysand's experience to be restored. In the analytic setting, how interpretations are "fed" to the patient according to "need" serves a containment function. The listening, the attention, the tone of voice, the understanding, and the misunderstandings that are received as information provide a containment which allows the analysand to begin anew and find, through relatedness, the constituents of aliveness. In this way, the "shell" of the second skin is replaced with a permeable cohesive skin that provides the means for taking in and letting out and, subsequently, internalization and identification.

For example, one patient described "finding" her analyst's face for the first time. In one session, she asked to sit for a few minutes, to be allowed to have the experience of looking that included "taking in," rather than the "staring" that previously warded off taking in. This is an indication that enough of a cohesive container had been internalized to allow integration to proceed. Later, this patient found the analyst's smell, which she described as "ambrosia," and she described the physical sensation of "eating" the analyst's smell. Sounds coming from the analyst would "tickle" her and evoke ebullient laughter. As a cohesive skin "takes shape," the inner space comes alive. A process of thawing occurs. This experience results in a sense of "self"—as one patient put it, the experience of being a person.

The thawing process and the creation of a cohesive boundary is accompanied by the expression of grief. Authentic contact with the analyst allows the original pain to be experienced. It is as if, over time, the tears melt the second skin exterior that has served as a protective shell. This mourning process indicates the separation from the skin of the mother. This is not Kleinian depressive anxiety associated with acknowledgment of destruction of the object. It indicates rather a giving up of the fantasy of omnipotent reparation and is thus a mourning for the loss of self and object to each other as they grow separate skins. A normal paranoid-schizoid-depressive constellation will then become apparent, and the analyst will be loved and hated and finally found as a person. Such a recognition marks a willingness to assume the appropriate role of child (dependency).

Profound terror often accompanies the grief that indicates integration. The terror relates to the original trauma. It is also the terror of what one patient called the "retarded child" who has been hidden in a cocoon created by the misappropriation of the parental role. This retarded child has turned away from dependency and learning through relationship. There is a recurrent return to the pathological organization as the patient experiences shame about the retarded child's existence. A despair with regard to the possibility of the rehabilitation of the retarded child must be acknowledged and accepted by both patient and analyst. When the analyst contains the despair, the retarded child can be included in the analysis and thereby be in relationship and accede to growth.

Summary

I have discussed a precocious organization in which addiction is used to sustain a fantasy of an internal space that can be omnipotently controlled. Addiction is said to arise out of a deficiency in the containment relationship of the mother/infant dyad, leading to the infant's formation of a second-skin which is fantasized as keeping both members of the dyad alive. Addiction is hypothesized as indicating "precocious growth" which does not allow for the development of a normal paranoid-schizoid-depressive constellation. A clinical example is presented and the state of addiction is described.

Addiction is said to arise out of the necessity to take responsibility for one's own psychological existence before one is equipped to do so. It is asserted that the analytic process can address the existence of a precocious paranoid-schizoid-depressive organization and facilitate the resumption of integrative processes. Experience pertaining to authentic relationship can then be restored, and responsibility for one's own being appropriately resumed.

NOTES

1. The controversy over the question of primary narcissism versus the existence of a separate ego from birth resolves itself in the concept of a skin-ego, in which the incipient ego formulates itself at the border, and thus is both separate and not separate, as the skin is in relation to the body.

2. Grotstein, reserving the term autistic exclusively for a neurological condition, characterizes the "autistic infant," as described by Tustin, as the "schizoid infant."
3. In a personal communication with Frances Tustin, she suggested that "separatedness" be used to specify a very early distinguishing of self from object, differentiated from later processes of separation as specified, for example, in Mahler's separation-individuation stages.

REFERENCES

Anzieu, D. (1989). *The skin ego*. New Haven & London: Yale University Press.
—— (1990). *Psychic Envelopes*. London: Karnac Books.
Bick, E. (1967). The experience of the skin in early object-relations. In: *Collected Papers of Martha Harris and Esther Bick*. Pertshire: Clunie Press, 1987, pp. 114-118.
Bion, W.R. (1962). Learning from Experience. London: Karnac Books, 1984.
—— (1967). *Second Thoughts. Selected Papers on Psychoanalysis*. London: Karnac Books, 1984.
Freud, S. (1923). *The Ego and the Id*. S.E., 1961, 19: 3-59. In: J. Strachey (Ed.), *Standard Edition of the Complete Psychological Works of Sigmund Freud*, 24 volumes. London: Hogarth Press & The Institute of Psycho-Analysis, 1953-1974.
Gabbard, G. (1991). Technical approaches to transference hate. In: L. B. Boyer and P. Giovacchini (Eds.), *Master Clinicians on Treating the Regressed Patient*. Northvale, NJ: J. Aronson, pp. 299-319.
Gaddini, E. (1992). *A Psychoanalytic Theory of Infantile Experience*. London & New York: Tavistock/Routledge.
Greenacre, P. (1953). *Trauma, Growth and Personality*. London: Hogarth Press.
Grinberg, L. (1990). *The Goals of Psychoanalysis*. London: Karnac Books.
Grotstein, J.S. (1991). Nothingness, meaningless, chaos, and the "black hole": III. Self-regulation and the background presence of primary identification. *Contemp. Psychoanal.*, 27(1), 1-33.
—— (1994). Notes on Fairbairn's metapsychology. In: J.S. Grotstein and D.B. Rinsley (Eds.). *Fairbairn and the Origins of Object Relations*. London: Free Association Books, 1994, pp. 112-148.
James, M. (1960). Premature ego development. Some observations on disturbances in the first three months of life. In: G. Kohon (Ed.), *The British School of Psycho-Analysis: The Independent Tradition*. London: Free Association Books, pp. 101-116.
Joseph, B. (1989). *Psychic Equilibrium and Psychic Change*. London: Tavistock/Routledge.

Kernberg, O. (1975). *Borderline Conditions and Pathological Narcissism*. Northvale, NJ: J. Aronson.

Klein, M. (1975). *The Writings of Melanie Klein, Vols. 1-4*. Edited by Roger Money-Kyrle in collaboration with Betty Joseph, Edna O'Shaughnessy and Hanna Segal. London: Hogarth Press.

Krystal, H. (1970). *Drug Dependence: Aspects of Ego Function*. Detroit: Wayne State University Press.

McDougall, J. (1989). *Theaters of the Body*. London: Free Association Books.

Meltzer, D.W. (1973). *Sexual States of Mind*. Perthshire: Clunie Press.

Meltzer, D.W., Brenner, J., Hoxter, S., Wedell, H., Wittenberg, I. (1975). *Explorations in Autism*. Perthshire: Clunie Press.

Ogden, T. (1989). *The Primitive Edge of Experience*. Northvale, NJ: J. Aronson.

Rey, H. (1994). *Universals of Psychoanalysis in the Treatment of Psychotic and Borderline States*. London: Free Association Books.

Rosenfeld, D. (1991). *The Psychotic Aspects of the Personality*. London: Karnac Books.

Tustin, F. (1981). *Autistic States in Children*. London & New York: Tavistock/ Routledge.

—— (1990). *The Protective Shell in Children and Adults*. London: Karnac Books.

Winnicott, D.W. (1958). *Through Paediatrics to Psycho-Analysis*. London: Hogarth Press.

—— (1965). *The Maturational Processes and the Facilitating Environment*. Madison, CT: International Universities Press.

Young, E. (1987). Co-alcoholism as a disease: Implications for psychotherapy. *J. Psychoactive Drugs*, 19(3), 257-268.

Young, E. (1991). The role of incest issues in relapse. *J. Psychoactive Drugs*, 22(2), 249-258.

924 Regal Road
Berkeley, California 94708
USA

JOURNAL OF MELANIE KLEIN AND OBJECT RELATIONS
Vol. 14, No. 2, December 1996

Recent Titles from
KARNAC BOOKS and CLUNIE PRESS

Donald MELTZER. *Sincerity and Other Works. Collected Papers of Donald Meltzer.* Edited by Alberto Hahn. London: Karnac Books, 1994, 590 pp. ISBN 1-85575-084-8.

SINCERITY AND OTHER WORKS brings together a collection of 34 papers by Donald Meltzer, which open up into a creative process covering the period from 1955 to 1989. Four papers have been written in collaboration with Esther Bick, Martha Harris, Mauro Mancia and Meg Harris Williams. The important problems of psychoanalytic theory and technique are approached in an elegant and concise style, where thoughts are rooted in clinical experience and return to it fertilized by a permanently renewed metapsychology. It is difficult to decide whether the greatest merit of this book is the spectrum it covers, the courage of an investigation which is never deterred by obstacles or the serene reflection with which the author approaches the issues of contemporary psychoanalysis. Only the reader can choose some of these or other alternatives but it is certain that (s)he will do so with passion and will not feel disappointed. Meltzer will leave everlasting impressions in the future of psychoanalysis.

✻ ✻ ✻

Eric H. RHODE, *Psychotic Metaphysics.* London: The Clunie Press & Karnac Books, 1994, 326 pp. ISBN 1-85575-074-0.

The threshold that M. Klein found to exist between the paranoid-schizoid and the depressive positions is the site of a series of transformations defined by W.R. Bion as a state of catastrophic change, and comparable to the stage in rites of passage, as described by Arnold van Gennep, in which initiates undergo an experience of psychic eclipse. With a wealth of clinical material, linking themes derived from psychotherapy, the arts, anthropology and philosophy, E. Rhode proposes that this turbulence, which logically precedes embodiment, is the impetus for the unique quality of human achievement. At the center of turbulence, mind begins to realize that it has gained power by robbing its good objects. It enters into a necessarily metaphysical and depressive exploration of psychotic iconography, in which an inadequate language of fetish and sign inhibits the emergence of symbols of love. It also discovers a geography of binary division, an underworld (as well as an overworld), to which it has banished its counterpart, a twin foetus and its mother, whom it must come to acknowledge as the rightful inheritors of life.

KARNAC BOOKS, 58 Gloucester Road, London SW7 4QY
THE CLUNIE PRESS, Old Ballechin, Strath Tay, Pertshire Scotland

Beyond the Infinite:
Psychotherapy with a Psychotic Child

Jeanne Magagna

The structure of time is inextricably linked with the concept of hope. In the beginning of the life of a baby there is hope, hope for a communion with the mother as a loving, protective, caring figure. Alongside this hope is a pre-conception that the breast will meet the baby's requirements to be nourished. As the baby grows and matures, holding on to this hope is both difficult and dangerous. Hope can be filled with too much greed to possess all of a mother's and father's life. Also, hope can be filled with a constitutional incapacity to tolerate the frustration of waiting for mother's reappearance. Hope can also be filled with rage at mother for not coming quickly enough, not being attuned to the baby's rhythm of communicating needs. Hope is then submerged under rage and disappointment with mother. Hope which promised a future of contentment then becomes despair. Without hope, there is no sense of the future. There is just the disappointing present, or the yearning for some moment in the past which was experienced as good.

In meeting a child who arrives for the initial session with his or her parents, I am acutely attuned to the sense of expectation that the child has in meeting me. In that first look I see hope, curiosity, anticipation that perhaps with this new person some different experience may occur. Alternatively, I see fear or even terror that something dreadful will certainly happen in my presence. I too have a sense of suspenseful anticipation as I get to know the child. In this first meeting I am the recipient of the child's current unconscious phantasies developed in past interactions with the mother, father and siblings. I am also me, with my personality, my inner world, consisting of flaws and capacities in the present, influencing the appearance of a particular configuration of phantasies in the child. What the future holds is uncertain. As a therapist I arrive with a hope that together we might repair some of the damage which has occurred internally, possibly in conjunction with conflictual external events.

JOURNAL OF MELANIE KLEIN AND OBJECT RELATIONS, 1996, 14(2), 197-222

Naturally the child's experience of time is apparent in the first session with the therapist. A child's sense of time changes considerably during the course of therapy. In presenting my psychotherapeutic work with a six year old psychotic child in four times a week therapy for three years, I shall contrast experiences of time in different phases of the therapy. The experience of time in a manic state of mind will be contrasted to an experience of time in depression and in depressive states of mind.

Mia, a child with many psychotic features, made me acutely aware of how distortions of time and space are apparent in the first session. At six, Mia was brought to the clinic by her parents because her teacher was worried about her living "in a world of her own." Everyone knew when Mia had arrived. She darted through the corridors shrieking. She was a lovely, robust little girl with brown curly hair. She had a hard muscular tone giving an impression of toughness.

Complaining that there was a large frightening man in the corner of the interview room, Mia constantly moved from one place to another. In the first family interview when no one responded to her complaints about the man invisible to them, she screamed at the hallucinated figure, "Bugger," "sod," "bastard!" This provoked distaste and alarm in the psychiatric meeting with the family. Mia teased and hit her twelve-year-old brother Rick. Rick was a focus of both Mia's and her mother's attention. Her mother whispered to him as a close confidant. Meanwhile, Mia's father was assertive and flamboyantly hypomanic in contrast to his withdrawn, subservient and depressed wife.

The family described how Mia was conceived in order that her brother "would not be left on his own with no one to care for him." Breast-fed until the fourth week when mother's milk dried up, Mia didn't cry much as a baby. Consequently, her mother said, she rarely felt the need to pick her up and cuddle her. At 10 months Mia was walking. Her mother encouraged Mia to draw for she never did like playing with toys. Sometimes she waved around a hard, sexy fashion model doll, but she never played with it.

The psychologist attempted to give Mia intelligence and achievement tests on two occasions, but said it was impossible to get any answers except nonsensical ones from her. Certainly her teachers felt Mia was not functioning within a normal range of intelligence. She could not concentrate and learned little in her year and a half at school. They said that she rarely responded to her own name and demanded that the teacher call her by different names. Once at a school bazaar Mia managed to escape from the adults, put on some clothes that were on sale and have her own clothes purchased.

Family life was chaotic with her father having frequent affairs. There was a history of violent rows between the older three family members. These rows resulted in broken doors, stitches on the mother's face, and a need for the mother to be present to protect the children from the father's frightening shouts. Mia's parents clearly needed assistance in handling their marital conflicts. Frequently her mother was too depressed and lonely to be actively concerned with Mia. At times Mia's father was absent from the home, apparently too preoccupied with his sexual partners and work which he used to relieve the "deadness" he complained about experiencing at home.

I embarked on four-time a week psychotherapy with Mia. This part of the treatment lasted three and a half years.

As I approach Mia, I see sores around her mouth and under her nose. Her face seems unattractive, particularly because of her dulled expression and her avoidance of eye contact. Mia's movements are extremely swift. Catching sight of me, Mia rushes toward me saying, "soft, good lady." A complete stranger to her, I am startled as she immediately strokes my grey lambswool jumper and eagerly demands, "Can I go with you now?" Hurriedly she grabs my hand, repeats "soft, good lady" and leaves her mother without even a glance to say goodbye.

Upon entering the therapy room, I give Mia a box of play materials and explain that the materials are for her to use during her time with me. Mia ignores the toys and hastily grabs the cellotape and all the crayons. She immediately begins a detailed drawing of the room and all its contents. She draws the chairs, the tables, the cellotape and then a detailed picture of me. The desk, the chair and I all occupy the same space. (See *Figure 1*: The Therapy Room.)

With mounting excitement Mia names the "objects" in the room. In her list she includes blond hair, grey eyes, knickers, table. The drawing of the objects and naming them to me meant Mia's attempt to understand and control them, and to make the place with me less frightening to her. Mia seriously observes, "You don't have pink skin." She then completes her list: Knickers, brown knickers filled with smellies and wees. Darting her eyes at me, Mia demands, "Pig, make grunting noises. I'm a lady."

Swiftly she removes every toy from the box while correctly naming the sheep, cow, lion and other animals she is dropping on the table. "I'm afraid of the man in the pink shirt!" she says. Subsequently, at lightning speed, she races out of the room into a tent in the waiting room. It takes me a second to reach her. As I do Mia shouts at me, "Pig! Frightened of you!"

Mia hastily grabs my hand and begs me to take her to the loo. I agree. Returning to the room she looks at me and remarks, "Man in the pink shirt. He's after me." She points at me and tries repeatedly to dash out of the

Figure 1. The Therapy Room

What part of the subject
in what state,
situated where in space and time,
does what,
with what motivation,
to what part of the object,
in what state,
situated where in space and time,
with what consequences for the
object and the subject?

Figure 2. Rey's Model of Thinking

room. This time I am more alert and firmly encourage her to remain inside the room until the end of the session. With a look of apparent pleasure Mia notices Turner's watercolor landscape entitled "Sunrise" hanging on the wall. Then she exclaims, "It's filled with smellies!" At this point the session ends and I return Mia to her mother. A few minutes later, the door bursts open. Mia is there shouting "pig" once again. She then races to the exit where her mother is standing.

Contemplating Mia's manic state, I ask myself, "What has happened to make everything go so fast in Mia's manic state?" Why are her emotions of love, fear and hate quickly reversible in seconds? It feels as though a hurricane has enveloped me in a swirl of confusing feelings. Finding a time to think about my own responses is essential before beginning another session with Mia. Dr. Rey's (1994) structure for thinking lends a depth to the process of examining Mia's manic relation to time and space. He recognizes the essentially spatial structure of the mind and its relation to objects which are spatially represented in the mind. Rey's developing consciousness of the structure of states of mind can be summed up as in *Figure 2*, Rey's Model of Thinking.

I used this model as a base for my review of the session with Mia. Mia was a baby who "didn't cry." Her depressed mother's milk dried up at four weeks. Mia exists in the sensori-motor stage of thinking. Her mind has easily permeable pores through which all outer stimuli beckon her, like the tune of the Pied Piper. As she touches my soft, wool jumper, she is dragged into a static sensuousness that obliviates her emotions and thoughts. My hair, eyes and jumper seem virtually equivalent to the toys, table and cellotape which she also names. The outer sensual qualities of objects all beckon her.

Mia attempts to "hold onto" a person immediately. All those laborious steps of taking time to get to know someone are skipped over as she grabs my hand and hastily claims that I am the "soft, good lady." She doesn't know my inner qualities, but since I am "soft" she assumes that I must be "good." Present is an omniscient certainty about who I am and a primitive omnipotent control through naming objects and pinning them down in a drawing. Obscured is waiting for the future with ordinary curiosity and anxiety regarding what might happen in the session.

The unheld, terrified infant, Mia, in a new space grabs the sensuous aspects of the "mother-therapist." Through sensuous looking and touching the "baby-Mia" attempts to hold on for dear life. Being overwhelmed with the sensuous qualities of the maternal object, she quickly intrudes beyond the space that baby a shares with its mother and enters into the primitive

Oedipal phantasies of mother in an exciting intercourse with the father. Only when I attempt to understand Mia's anxieties about being with a stranger in a new place is she able to say, "You're not pink." However, this quality of "not-pinkness," meaning "not too exciting," is quickly lost in the presence of Mia's wish to possess immediately all that the mother had including the sensuous, sexual relationship with the father. The mother is not permitted time away to be with daddy. Rapidly the "hallucinated pink man" returns to the room and is located within me. In other words, the "soft, good lady" is spoiled by the exciting, hated and terrifying "pink man" and becomes a "pig."

There is no separation in time of the "nurturing, feeding mother" from the phantasies which quickly become sensual, sexual and anal in quality. In her unintegrated state, Mia flits between one state of mind to another in rapid succession. There exists one form of splitting: mother is good, father is bad, but only for a second. Then good and bad become confused leading to a monstrous "pig" containing Mia's projections. This greed is stimulated by Mia's lack of inner containment. Sensuous erotization is Mia's defence against the pain of dependence and loss of the feeding object. The manic race involving nonstop touching of objects, and flitting through different activities are designed to flee from the primitive persecutory anxieties and terror of the "hallucinated monster pink man." Any potential emotional rather than sensuous relationship with me is superficial and quickly loses value. This is the world of two dimensional time and two dimensional adherence to the surface of objects described by Meltzer and Tustin.

In ordinary human experience, over time, there is a continuity of emotional experience rather than the roller coaster of excited and terrifying states of mind in which Mia exists. The continuity of emotional experience in time is provided through the containing presence of the external mother and father. The containing parental presence becomes internalized to form the child's internal psychic structure. Manic racing through time is replaced by an ordinary use of time when there is an internal psychic structure holding Mia's feelings sufficiently long to be perceived and given consideration.

Blistering of the Skin

By the third week of therapy, Mia experiences separation from me as being dropped from a state of at one-ness into a state of being torn off, bruised, and blistered. My heart cries out as I see the futile attempts which Mia makes to interrupt the passage of time leading to the end of the session.

Initially Mia starts wearing lipstick and carrying a small bag containing her mother's eye shadow, lipstick, rouge, mascara, perfume, and nail varnish. Her face is carefully made up like a grown-up mother going to a party. Alternatively, she spends time before she leaves the session, making up her face so that she has a "beautiful face." At other times, she puts glue on her feet, tries to stick them to the floor, and continually checks to see if they have stuck. There is to be no "baby" experiencing the passage of time away from the "mother-therapist."

In the following excerpts from a session you can see how Mia's search to get into and adhere to the protective skin of the "mother-therapist" also takes the shape of covering herself with plasticine:

Mia pours water all over the room, throws and scatters her toys. She then begins rocking back and forth. She seems very sad, not knowing what to do. Mia then collects plasticine pieces from amongst the debris and stands near me saying, "I'm putting plasticine all over myself." She labels a piece of the plasticine "the desk bit" and tries to stick it into the bottom of her feet. When she is unsuccessful, she tries using glue to make the "desk bit" adhere to her feet. Shortly afterwards Mia collects more plasticine and begins sticking it all over her body saying, "I'm putting Ms. Storey all over me." Mia is serious, slow moving and quiet. I feel that she is slightly desperate. Mia repeats this in subsequent sessions adding felt tip to cover her navel and arms. During this same period she does stick figure drawings such as in Figure 3.

The plasticine cover, the felt tip color and the "make-up mummy beautiful face" are part of Mia's attempt to retreat from any experience of being a kind of stick figure without much inner substance, flesh or even human shape. The covers in which Mia attempts to reside are evasions of some terrible sense of fragmentation and potential sense of loss of the therapist-mother. Mia's aim is to obliterate time, a sense of waiting, an experience of psychic terror and pain when a separate person.

But, the experience of rage and hurt is emerging. The skin as a concrete locus of Mia's separation soreness is particularly evident at the end of many sessions. Frequently she does not want to leave the sessions. When I firmly insist that it is time to go, Mia tries to scratch me, rip my tights, kick me and pull my hair. In this way I am to concretely experience the flayed skin sensation, the blistering skin, the hurt which Mia experiences when I say, "it's time to go."

During the fifth week Mia spends some of the sessions curled up under the blanket on the couch. I feel she is beginning to become painfully aware of her sense of loss, her feeling of bodily damage as we part. She feels helpless without a sturdy internal psychic structure enabling her to consider that there will be another session and another. This internal rhythm of safety could hold her flood of despair and terror arising through fragmentation of the self in the time apart. I talk about Mia wanting a "blanket-mummy" to hold her together and make her feel safe. At the end, Mia cries pleading that she does not want to go. Later in the corridor, as she meets her mother, she becomes very subdued and begins sobbing. Mia complains that her mother has not brought her scarf. This is the very first day I have seen Mia crying. As she cries in front of her mother, I feel "Now there is a crying baby, a baby crying for a 'blanket-mummy' to hold her pain and protect her."

For a moment the obliteration of time through sensuousness ceases. There is an acute experience of an emotional point which is held still. There is a time and some internal space in which Mia feels sadness and fear of being without a protective cover. Emerging in Mia is a new concept of · "mother," the concept of a mother who can experience and understand her sadness and fear of loss of protection.

Mia's new concept of mother transforms her basic structure of time. There is now the possibility of a sense of loss followed by a reunion, a sense of loss with a limit. Timelessness, the sense of infinite loss, can be gradually replaced by waiting for a reunion with the "lost mother." In time apart from the" mother-therapist," Mia can begin to perceive a future reunion as being the end to the present painful sense of loss.

Around the third and fourth week, it is clear that Mia is more vehemently using me as a kind of "dump" into which she evacuates parts of her blistered self. For example:

At the beginning of one session she immediately rushes to the jug of water. Pouring water on the couch, she declares, "Pouring water on you bed." She then takes off her shoes and socks. Racing to the desk, she grabs her box and dumps all its contents on the floor saying, "I'm messing up your room again." She pours glue all over and attempts to kick me. When I restrain her, she bites me.

But then she steps on a piece of fence and cries complaining, "It pricked me." When I describe her feeling that she has messed the inside of the mummy and now she feels she is being pricked and made to cry, Mia responds, "Yes, it hurts me."

In the next session Mia puts the fence pieces in a bucket and places them under the couch along with other hard toys. She explains, "It's so they won't hurt." Emerging for the first time is a concept of a space where the bad bits can be stored. This session is also marked by Mia's uncharacteristic crying and verbal communication about feeling hurt. Now there is a "mother as dumping place" into which Mia can expel some unbearable destructive and hurt feelings. After the painful and bad parts of experience can be stored it becomes possible to see the development of a space to protect "good parts."

At this stage, feelings and thoughts are still fragmentary and dominated by an emphasis on sensory concretization of her experience. This is apparent when in her sixth week of therapy Mia arrives for the first time with a watch on. She requests that I take care of her "ticker" in my drawer. Shortly afterwards she asks me to keep her large red button earrings safe in my drawer during the session. I feel that I am to be a kind of "special secure place" for those parts of herself that she wishes to protect from the chaos created by her continual messing of the room. There is just a hint of Mia's developing internalization of a "talking mummy with a protective space inside her." Mia alternates between messing the entire room and lying completely under the couch cover using my words as an additional blanket to wrap round herself.

Mia has little capacity for symbolic thought. For this reason she concretizes her notion of time passing and future time when we will meet again and she can listen to me. She does this in her asking me to keep her watch and earrings safe. At this time, Mia cannot keep this notion of our time together safely inside her. The beginning of each session recapitulates the internal process that has occurred during the separation from me. Rage about separation and subsequent fragmentation of the introjected experience of being understood by me creates internal chaos. Upon entering the room Mia regularly feels compelled to throw toys and water all over. In this way she thrusts her internal chaos and rage into me. After I receive this chaos, Mia can begin to elaborate on other experiences she has.

The minute there is a greater sense of my having a good protective function, Mia becomes worried about the time. She greets me worrying, "What time is it? When will it be time to go?" She curls up under the couch cover and then pops up, rushes over to me and explains that she wants to "push the button on my head." She wants to push the button on my head in order to take control of my speaking and thinking functions. I suggest that Mia is trying to turn me on and off at will.

This is primitive omnipotent control showing me that she cannot tolerate the terror of being in a dependent relation to a good figure. She immediately

Figure 3. Stick Figure

Figure 4. The Bus Conductor

has to flee to be in control. Increased dependence on the mother-therapist is heralded by more severe anxieties about being helpless outside the sessions. Mia cries plaintively when she leaves this session.

At this time of more dependence on me, Mia also begins to experience sleeping difficulties. She says she likes sleeping in my room and would like to sleep in my room every night, because my room does not have cracks in it like her room does. The external object, the therapist, gives her the feeling of a soothing protective space, a space without cracks. However, outside the therapy Mia feels she is left with a faulty, cracked, internal psychic container which does not protect her.

In the sixth week of therapy, Mia also places a big red button inside a bus which she draws. She indicates that the woman in the bus could "press the button so the bus would stop." She adds that "the button is to make sure that nobody falls out." Here she is expressing her desire for the mummy as a kind of protector, a kind of "bus-mummy cover" who holds her in mind and does not let her drop. Also present, however, is a very monstrous looking "bus driver." She now has a sense of a daddy infringing on her relation to the mother. In subsequent sessions the drawings indicate that the "daddy" threatens to leave her feeling dropped out from the cocoon of the "bus-mummy covering."

What is important though is the emergence of this figure who is able to put a time limit to experience, either good or bad. In a very primitive way, this limit on time with mother is felt to be the "role of the father." The structure of time with the limiting role of the father is depicted through the button to press to get out of the bus and a bus conductor. (See *Figure 4*: Bus Conductor.)

Differing meanings are now being ascribed by Mia to her notion of a "time limit." Mia's terror of being dropped into an abyss at the end of session and rage toward an already violent external father create the "monster father" who enforces cruel limits and drops people out thoughtlessly. This contrasts with another image of limits which is the button which the mother presses with a more kindly role of ensuring that people can get out safely from "inside the mummy" and don't ride inside the "protective bus-mummy" forever. Of course, in the unconscious, infinite varieties of the protective or cruel father putting time limits exist.

In psychotherapy asymmetrical logic and symmetric logic challenge one another. The presence of an internal containing mother permitting thinking to take place, allows Mia to feel that just because there is a time limit, it doesn't mean that I am with a monster who is cruel to her. However, when feelings become too extreme and violent, the deeper symmetrical logic takes precedence: "There is a time limit. People who put time limits are monsters.

The therapist is a monster."

Mia drew these pictures when she experienced the monstrous time-limiting figure. Before she drew the witch she said she hated me because I said "No." (See *Figures 5-8.*)

The question is what happens with the experience of the cruelty of the time limits arising after the emergence of a sense of dependence on an important protective mother figure? How does a substantial transformation of the personality structure of Mia take place so that the "hallucinated monster man" or the "frightening witch-mother" do not reappear each time Mia's wishes for nonstop living inside the protective covers are thwarted?

As Mia develops, her singing begins to be a bridge between concrete sensation dominated experiences and symbolic thought. At times her singing blots me out, but at other times the singing indicates acknowledgement of absence and an attempt to make an internal mother come more vividly alive. Her song about a beggar in need indicates a complexity of thought and feeling which she is not yet able to put into words. Then having asked about the number of minutes left, Mia attempts to measure out the time by singing the scale, "do, re, mi." Time has become quantifiable, linked with music and my American money, and S the initial of my surname Storey used at that time. She is beginning to quantify time with an awareness of its rhythm, pace—going fast, going slow, and having musical notes linked with the sounds of my voice. Accompanying this quantification of time is the sense of intervals, like the breaks in therapy. This sense of time and rhythm is repeatedly illustrated in a series of drawings she makes over two weeks proceeding the Christmas holidays. The Christmas holiday calendar which I make is linked by her to the musical scale. Obvious through this drawing is Mia's awareness of the "father conductor" of the flow of the mother's milk-voice-understanding and the tempo of the sessions. Still present at times in the face of the termination of therapy is Mia's wish to replace the father as the conductor of the music of the mother's voice. The different rhythmic movements of the lines on a series of drawings seem to represent Mia's recreation of the rhythm and flow of her therapy music, the intervals and days of the sessions and her wish for an endless flow of sessions. Present, though, is an acknowledgement of the father's role as the creator, along with the mother, of the mother's internal music. (See *Figures 9-14.*)

In reviewing the sessions, I begin to ask myself the question, "When does Mia's copying of concrete sensory details move toward creative symbolic representation?" My tentative answer is that when there is the threat of "time apart" and Mia's destructive self is in a rage against the "conductor-father" who puts an end to the therapy music, several different situations can occur:

Figure 5. Witch Breast Mother

Figure 6. Two Witches and Pot

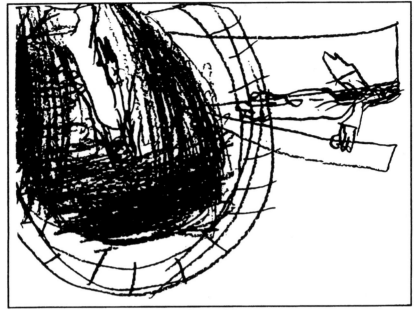

Figure 7. Dead Person

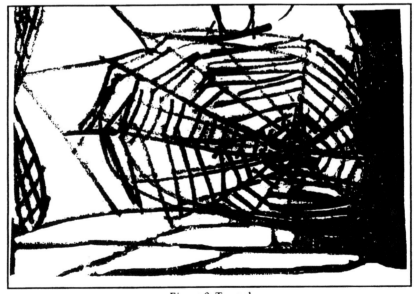

Figure 8. Tunnel

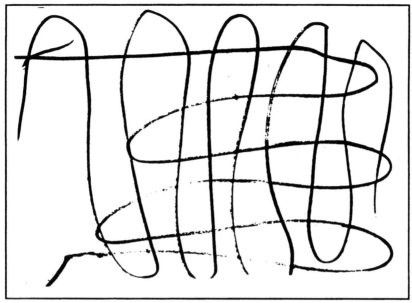

Figure 9. Music Drawing

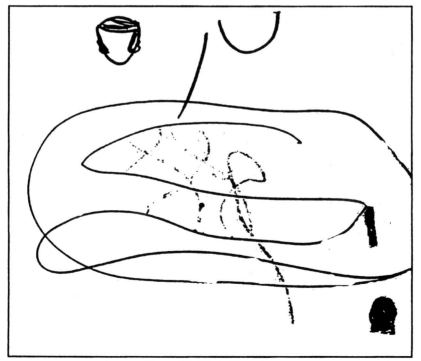

Figure 10. Music Drawing

Figure 11. Music Drawing

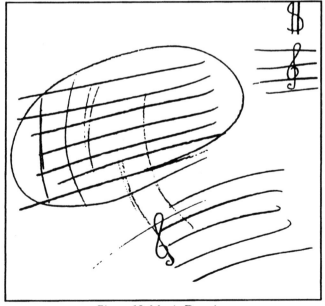

Figure 12. Music Drawing

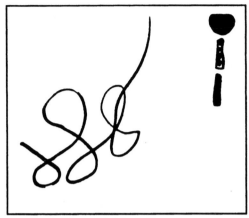

Figure 13. Music Drawing

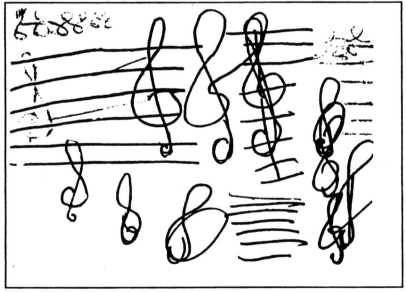

Figure 14. Music Drawing

1. In a regressive stop the "conductor-father" becomes hallucinated as the "terrible man" in the room, in an attempt to prevent his introjection and spoiling the good but idealized mother in a good internal space.

2. She slips into being projectively identified with a mother, but now she is no longer a mother preoccupied with her makeup and looks, but rather a mother who is wheeling a baby around in a pram, looking after a baby.

3. Following a destructive attack on the disappearing "mother-therapist" there is an upsurge of loving, reparative wishes mitigating Mia's hate. When this predominance of Mia's love mitigates her jealous attack, Mia produces these more symbolic drawings. The flow of the lines suggests that she is allowing thought and feeling to become integrated in a free and more creative way.

Thus, it is possible to envisage "time-apart" as being either a moment for Mia's regression or her development.

Transformation in Time

As assessment of therapeutic progress of the child in therapy involves an examination of the changing nature of the time limiting role of the father, which permits the mother-therapist to have a creative space to join the father and other babies. The role of the father also ensures a regular rhythm of therapy sessions, at a particular time, for a particular period. Near the end of treatment there is a resurgence of love and the capacity to appreciate the notion of time to grow up supported by the protective role of the father enabling limits to be maintained. There is also often a resurgence of hate and the potential perils of the time-limit proposed by the "end of therapy."

I shall now describe the end of three years of four-time a week psychotherapy to show the fluctuations in Mia's concept of time.

Knowing therapy is ending in a few months time, Mia arrives pushing a pram with a baby doll inside. The previous week she brought a live kitten from home into the session. Mia says that I am an "old-fashioned cushion" and when questioned about what that means she says, "It is smelly and wrinkled." I describe how Mia feels there is a nice, fresh young mummy looking after a new baby, I seem to be the old mummy, a kind of old grandmother. I wonder if she is having difficulty letting me remain a good lively mummy-therapist, for fear that there will be another child following her time in therapy with me. About half-way through the session, Mia looks at me with amazement, smiles with a lovely expression on her face and says, "You have the lovely green silk blouse on." She says she would like to touch the collar and sit on my lap, but she remains seated across from me simply staring at me with a contemplative, serene expression on her face. I describe how she feels grateful for the experience of being understood by me. She feels the "beauty of the good mummy."

At this moment Mia seems to have stopped attacking the goodness of the mummy-therapist, robbing her by stealing the capacity to mother the baby. After some time in the session thinking with me, she is filled with awe, in the presence of the beauty of the object and love for the object and its resilience. Mia's experience now shows significant signs of being trans-formed from simply having a sensuous appreciation of the object which prompts adherence and intrusion into the "mother's skin." Now she feels the love and the passion necessary for creative endeavors of any sort to emerge.

It is around this time that Mia begins showing her transition from clinging to the immediate sensuous present to allowing creative experiences to emerge, and take her beyond the immediately perceived present. She yelled at me complaining that I don't really love her, I just love myself. She then asks me why I am looking so worried, feeling that my face is all screwed up. She says my eyelashes are like spiders, my teeth like pointed spears, my eyes like footballs, my neck like a tree trunk. This is followed by her saying, "No, you are not really like that." Then she transforms my "tree trunk neck" into a tree with flowing branches. (See *Figure 16*.)

This drawing is followed in a subsequent session by Mia saying that she thinks I have a child already lined up to be with me during the time she has been with me. She thinks that I am going to see this child forever and that I will take the child home with me. A series of sessions then occurred in which Mia tries to break the window and hits me.

Mia seems to allow me to have my therapeutic capacities when apart from her, but she wants to imprison me in my therapy room so that I will have no future except as a therapist. Example from the 33rd month (three months prior to ending):

Mia asked me if I remember the previous day's session when she put me in a prison "forever" with her. Then she wants to imprison me in a corner of the room farthest from the door saying that she is going to lock me in and

Figure 15. Rhythm of Feelings

Figure 16. Tree

only she can get out. I say she can tell me what she feels now. She says she is going to leave me all the mess and I can clean up. She is going to have a fantastic feast and I'm not invited. Mia then covers me with the couch cover and says that my eyes are to see beautiful things with and I can use my mouth to talk, but the rest of my body is old, mouldy and rotting and my head is covered with "old grey hairs."

I describe how Mia sees the future. Yesterday she talked of the "mother" with a lovely white mummy breast who took care of babies in a good way. Today she is imprisoning me so that I can have no future with the daddy, no babies, no other patients. I am to be HER therapist and ONLY a therapist. She feels this is the only way the mother-therapist can remain forever good inside her.

Mia recounts how she has had two dreams, one is a dream of my being a prisoner locked up with only bread and water, with only my head showing. The other dream is of my dying and going to the devils who burn me up. I am only ashes.

Intimations of the Future When Ending Therapy

During the last three months of therapy, the ending of therapy and a sense of our future lives dominate Mia's thinking. For a moment she contemplates the notion of being a growing girl.
Excerpts from the 36th month:

Mia states that she is growing up and that she is going to wear dresses from now on. Wearing dresses implies that she is relinquishing her place of trying to be daddy with the mummy-therapist. She looks calm and very pleased as she says, "Do you remember when I was seven? Do you remember when I was eight?" She implies by her calmness that she has outgrown all her wild messing of me and the room.

This emphasis on growing up and being able to separate from the mother-therapist immediately brings into play notions of the "new baby," the magician Oedipal father who takes the "little girl from her mother" and the little girl left out in the cold, running for safety to her mother. As she draws this picture she says that I am not allowed to say "why, mummy, daddy, baby, or think." In other words, it is difficult to contemplate these issues of separateness from the mother, allowing mother the possibility of more patient-babies in the future. Yet the basis of her future feminine identity is identifying with the mother who is allowed her procreative capacities. A brief glimpse of this is in the drawing made right near the end of therapy (37th month) the "mummy" allowed to be pregnant and to have a baby. (See *Figure 17.*)

The problem of the future for Mia ending therapy remains the same as for the baby thinking of the future when mother puts her to bed for the night. How can the "baby-Mia" allow the mother-therapist her freedom to have a life with the father, with other children? At this point she imprisons the mother, burns the mother with her rage and then there is no sense of the future, only the death of the object. Hate and possessiveness are feelings easier to experience than the pain of loss of the therapist.

In retrospect, I would say that a much longer time in therapy is needed for such a very ill child to consolidate any internal developments made in the course of therapy. How the patient will live in the future is always filled with some uncertainty. What I do know though is that by the end of therapy, Mia had gained an appreciation of her responsibility for trying to protect her good internal mother from her possessiveness and rage. Mia wrote as follows: (See *Figure 18.*)

She has a notion that I had given her three and a half years of my life to help her to grow up. She also acknowledges that in some ways she has grown to be nice and in some ways she is still nasty. The future is determined by how Mia will be nurtured and understood and how she will allow me to have a life apart from her and forgive me for what we were not able to do together in therapy to foster her psychological development. Hope for the future is really based on recognizing and protecting the goodness of the internal mother. Protection of the internal mother comes through having sufficient love to forgive the internal mother and father and allow them freedom to be a procreative couple.

Time for termination of therapy should come about in the therapist's mind when this possibility of preserving the good internal parents arises in the child. However, as in the ending of Mia's therapy, when such total internal destruction of the good object occurs and there is no possibility of going through the mourning process, the therapist needs to reconsider the notion of "time for the termination of therapy." Whatever external crises arise, hope for the future can exist only through taming of the destructive feelings so that the internal parents can be restored to goodness and remain understanding and protective throughout life. (See *Figure 19.*)

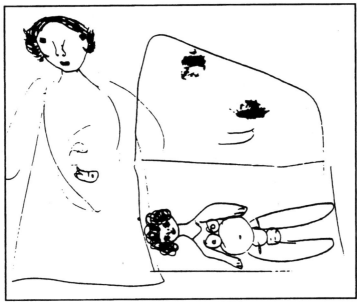

Figure 17. Mother and Baby

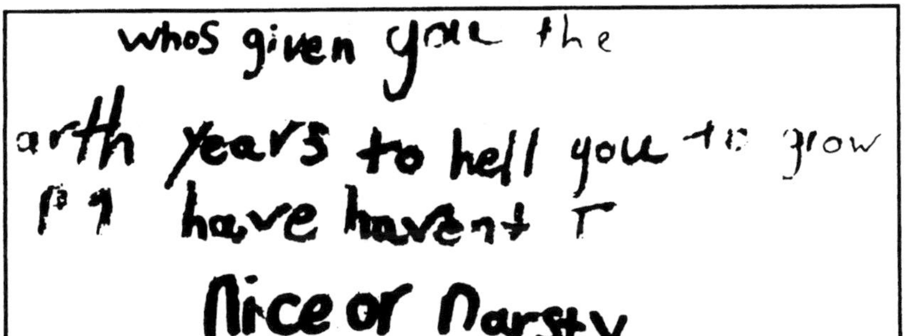

whos given you the
arth years to hell you to grow
have havent
Nice or Narsty

Figure 18. Nice or Nasty

Figure 19. Lovely Woman

Conclusion

Until there is a perception of a good object, life remains hazardous and unpredictable. When separate from the good object life continues to be hazardous and unpredictable until there is an introjection of the good object. The introjection of the good object and the maintaining of its goodness while allowing the primary object to be absent, produce three profoundly important transformations in the child's experience of time (Colarusso, 1979).

First, the child's sense of time becomes more self-contained and internalized. Gradually, time becomes less dependent on the presence or absence of the mother. Although the child's sense of time appears more autonomous, it is still largely related to the goodness or badness of the internalized mother. For example, if the child's rage against the absent object is too intense, the absent good object becomes a dying object. For example, there can be the fear that mother has died in a crash or drowned when she is away from the child. In this situation the child's experiences the waiting period as infinitely long until mother returns intact. If the child does not attack the external mother for being away and also allows her the freedom to be with the father and other children or her work, the child is able to hold onto a good internal object. Time away from mother does not seem so long for the "good mother inside" can be depended upon in mother's absence.

Second, with the endurance of the good internal object, past, present, and future begin to have some continuity as a psychic experience. The presence of the good internal object allows using the experience of the past to think about the present situation and contemplate the future. In this way, past, present, and future are all of interest and present in the conversation and thinking of the child.

Third, the child's identification with the internalized good object allows it an independent existence in the common time-space continuum. In this way the frustrations associated with time can be endured and mastered. Also, hope for the future can be maintained.

The sense of time is reflected in the language of a young child (Ames, 1946). "Soon" suggesting a sense of future by connoting waiting or delay is usually first heard by around 18 months of age. "Soon" is used knowingly when the child is around 24 months. "Tomorrow" is not verbalized spontaneously until the child is around 30 months and then it is expressed only after "today" has been expressed. "Yesterday" appears around 36 months of age. "Now" and "when" also appear between 18 and 36 months.

In her therapy, Mia seems to follow a similar sequence of relating to time, but first she goes through a sequence of severe depression in which she feels the torture to which she is exposed will last an eternity. Her sense of destruction and consequent despair is implied by the nonstop messing of my room and her images of death.

When the inner object is destroyed, there is no personal development. Depression is the result. In depression the inner feeling of time stops. There is no sense of the future. This sense of no future is often linked with the child's sadistic desire to perpetuate the suffering of others. Of course, the child's sadism may in part be connected with a destructive and extremely disappointing external environment. The sense of time is always connected with one's inner emotional life and never an independent unit.

If hope is directed solely toward a requirement for an external event to change rather than on the capacities of the good internal object, the adult is left in danger of facing devastating despair. The child is dependent on external figures to develop internally and hence more at risk of facing despair. As a therapist I try to alleviate the child's despair and provide hope for the child's future. Hope for the child's future is based on the security provided by the capacities of the good internal object to look after the self.

REFERENCES

Ames, L.S. (1946). The development of the sense of time in the young child. *J. Genetic Psychol.*, *18*, 97-125.
Colarusso, C. (1979). The development of time sense–From birth to object constancy. *Int. J. Psycho-Anal.*, *60*, 243-251.
Rey, H. (1994). *Universals of Psychoanalysis*. London: Free Associations Books.

Great Ormond Street Hospital
for Children NHS Trust
Great Ormond Street
London WC1N 3JH
England

JOURNAL OF MELANIE KLEIN AND OBJECT RELATIONS
Vol. 14, No. 2, December 1996

NOTES ON CONTRIBUTORS

DR. JAMES S. GROTSTEIN is Clinical Professor of Psychiatry at UCLA School of Medicine and Training/Supervising Analyst at the Los Angeles Psychoanalytic Institute and the Psychoanalytic Center of California. He is in private practice in West Los Angeles.

JEANNE MAGAGNA is a Consultant Child Psychotherapist at the Great Ormond Street Hospital for Children, London.

NEIL MAIZELS is a psychotherapist in private practice in Melbourne, Australia.

DR. ENID B. YOUNG is a graduate of the Psychoanalytic Institute of Northern California. She is in private practice in Berkeley and San Francisco, California.

New Titles from DUNOD ÉDITEUR

Didier ANZIEU, *Créer. Détruire*. Paris: Dunod Éditeur, 1996. 280 pp.
ISBN 2-04-015796-4.

This volume represents the culmination of an intellectual life centered around the concept of *creative psychic work*. As in the *Skin Ego* (1985; English edition, 1989), Didier ANZIEU has assembled articles from journals and collective volumes. The book contains 19 chapters divided in three parts:

- The double face: negative and destructive, but also positive and productive of any kind of creative work
- The case of Beckett, the writer
- The discovery and development of the Skin-ego

DIDIER ANZIEU is member of l'Association Psychanalytique de France and Professeur émérite at l'Université de Paris X Nanterre.

* * *

Patrice PAVIS. *Dictionnaire du théâtre*. 3rd ed. Paris: Dunod Éditeur, 1996. 622 pp. 178FF.

This is an entirely new and updated edition of the dictionary. The previous two editions (1980 and 1987) have been translated into Chinese, Hebrew, Korean, Polish, Sloven, Spanish and Russian. The present edition is a veritable compendium of some 600 terms on the history, theory and practice of the theater. Each entry comprises:

- a definition
- a review of the subject
- bibliographical references

This dictionary covers the dramatic art, texts and discourse, actors and characters, genres and forms, directing and staging, esthetics and semiology. It provides definitions and explanations of key-notions and is abundantly illustrated with examples from classical theater and contemporary directing.

PATRICE PAVIS is Professor of Theater Studies at l'Université de Paris VIII.

Orders: Ideal Foreign Books, Inc., 132-10 Hillside Avenue, Richmond Hill, NY 11418

Foreign rights: Mme Maryvonne Vitry, 15, rue Gossin, F-92541 Montrouge Cedex

Spanish, Portuguese rights: Sra M. Vallat, Maldonadas, 9 - 2° dcha, E - 28005 Madrid

BOOKS RECEIVED

ANZIEU, D. *Le Moi-peau.* Paris: Dunod. 1994. 254 pp.

ANZIEU, D. *Le Penser. Du Moi-peau au Moi-pensant.* Paris: Dunod. 1994. 180 pp.

ANZIEU, D. *Créer. Détruire.* Paris: Dunod. 1996. 280 pp.

ANZIEU, D., HAAG, G., TISSERON, S., LAVALLÉE, G., BOUBLI, M., Lassègue, J. *Les contenants de Pensée.* Paris: Dunod. 1993. 212 pp.

BOURGUIGNON, A., COTET, P., LAPLANCHE, J., ROBERT, F. *Traduire Freud.* Paris: Presses Universitaires de France. 1989. 382 pp.

CAVE, D. *Mircea Eliade's Vision for a New Humanism.* New York & Oxford: Oxford University Press, 1993. 218 pp.

DUPRIEZ, B. *A Dictionary of Literary Devices. Gradus, A-Z.* Translated and adapted by A.W. Halsall. Toronto & Buffalo: University of Toronto Press. 1991. 546 pp.

EISSLER, K.R. *Three Instances of Injustice.* Madison, CT: International Universities Press. 1993. 265 pp.

ELLENBERGER, H.F. *Beyond the Unconscious. Essays of Henri F. Ellenberger in the History of Psychiatry.* Introduced and edited by M.S. Micale. Princeton, NJ: Princeton University Press. 1993. 416 pp.

SIGMUND FREUD - SÁNDOR FERENCZI. Briefwechsel. Band I/1. 1908 bis 1911. Herausgegeben von E. Brabant, E. Falzeder und P. Giampieri-Deutsch unter der wissenschaft-lichen Leitung von A. Haynal. Transkription von I. Meyer-Palmedo. Wien, Köln & Weimar: Böhlau Verlag. 1993. 446 pp. (Book received courtesy of Mark Paterson and Associates, England.)

SIGMUND FREUD - SÁNDOR FERENCZI. Briefwechsel. Band I/2. 1912-1914. Herausgegeben von E. Brabant, E. Falzeder und P. Giampieri-Deutsch unter der wissenschaftlichen Leitung von A. Haynal. Transkription von I. Meyer-Palmedo. Wien, Köln & Weimar: Böhlau Verlag. 1993. 328 pp.

SIGMUND FREUD - SÁNDOR FERENCZI. Correspondence. 1908-1914. Edité par E. Brabant, E. Falzeder et P. Giampieri-Deutsch sous la direction d'André Haynal. Transcrit par I. Meyer-Palamedo. Traduit par S. Aacher-Wiznitzer, J. Dupont, S. Hommel, C. Knoll-Froissart, P. Sabourin, F. Samson, P. Thèves et B. This. Paris: Calman-Lévy. 1992. 648 pp. (Book received courtesy of Mark Patterson and Associates, England.)

SIGMUND FREUD Briefe an Wilhelm Fliess. 1887-1904. Ungekürzte Ausgabe

Herausgegeben von J.F. Masson. Deutsche Fassung von M. Scröter. Transkription von G. Fichtner. Frankfurt am Main: S. Fischer Verlag. 1986. 614 pp.

GROTSTEIN, J.S., RINSLEY, D.B. (Eds.). *Fairbairn and the Originis of Object Relations*. New York & London: The Guilford Press. 1994. 350 pp.

ETCHEGOYEN, R. H. *The Fundamentals of Psychoanalytic Technique*. Translated by P. Pitchon. Foreword by R.S. Wallerstein. With a chapter by G. Klimovsky. London & New York: Karnac Books. 1991. 864 pp.

KAËS, R. (Ed.), *Les voies de la Psyché. Hommage à Didier Anzieu*. Paris: Dunod. 1994. 548 pp.

MEHLER J.A., ARGENTIERI, S., CANESTRI, J. *La Babele dell'Inconscio. Lingua madre e lingua straniere nella dimensione psicoanalitica*. Milano: Raffaello Cortina Editore. 1990. 388 pp.

MELTZER, D. *Sincerity and Other Works. Collected Papers of Donald Meltzer*. Edited by Alberto Hahn. London: Karnac Books, 1994. 590 pp.

PAVIS, P. *Dictionnaire du théâtre*. 3rd ed. Paris: Dunod. 622 pp.

PETOT, J.-M. *Mélanie Klein. Premières découvertes et premier système. 1919-1932*. Paris: Dunod, 1979. 376 pp.

PETOT, J.-M. *Mélanie Klein. Le moi et le bon object. 1932-1960*. Paris: Dunod. 1982. 304 pp.

RHODE, E. *Psychotic Metaphysics*. Foreward by D. Meltzer. Oxford: The Clunie Press. London: Karnac Books. 1994. 326 pp.

RICKETTS, M.L. *Mircea Eliade. The Romanian Roots. 1907-1945*. Boulder: East European Monographs. (Distributed by Columbia University Press.) 1988. 2 vols. 1460 pp.

SPEZIALE BAGLIACCA, R. *On the Shoulders of Freud. Freud, Lacan, and the Psychoanalysis of Phallic Ideology*. Translated by D.E.W. Jones. New Brunswick, NJ & London: Transaction Publishers, 1991, 98 pp.

ARTICLES NOTICED

Athanassiou, C. L'apport de l'analyse de l'enfant à l'analyse de l'adulte: Le perspective kleiniene. [What child analysis contributes to the analysis of the adult: The Kleinian perspective.] *Rev. Franç. Psychanal.*, 1994, 58(3), 831-837. [Fren.]

Bacon, R. Paranoid knowledge. *Free Assn.*, 1995, 5(33, Pt. 1), 1-46.

Balenci, M. Sul concetto di angoscia reale in Freud, Anna Freud e Melanie Klein. [The concept of realistic anxiety in Freud, Anna Freud and Melanie Klein.] *Giornale Storico di Psicologia Dinamica.* 1993, 17(34), 45-60. [Ital.]

Berke, J.H & Schneider, S. Antithetical meanings of "the breast". *Int. J. Psycho-Anal.*, 1994, 75(3), 491-498.

Blackwell, D., Bell, D. & Dartington, T. Clinical commentary XVI. *Br. J. Psychother.*, 1993, 10(2), 253-269.

Blechner, M.J. Projective identification, countertransference, and the "maybe-me". *Contemp. Psychoanal.*, 1994, 30(3), 619-631.

Bleger, J. Die psychoanalyse des psychoanalytischen Rahmens. [Psychoanalysis of the psychoanalytic framework.] *Forum der Psychoanalyse: Zeitschrift für klinische Theorie & Praxis*, 1993, 9(3), 268-280.

Blomfield, O.H. The essentials of psychoanalysis. *Austral. New Zealand J. Psychia.*, 1993, 27(1), 86-100.

Boris, H.N. The self too seen. *Contemp. Psychoanal.*, 1994, 30(1), 101-113.

Boris, H.N. About time. *Contemp. Psychoanal.*, 1994, 30(2), 301-322.

Britton, R. Publication anxiety: Conflict between communication and affiliation. *Int. J. Psycho-Anal.*, 1994, 75(5-6), 1213-1224.

Britton, R. & Steiner, J., Interpretation: Selected fact or overvalued idea? *Int. J. Psycho-Anal.*, 1994, 75(5-6), 1069-1078.

Clarke, G. Notes towards an object-relations approach to cinema. *Free Assn.*, 1994, 4(31, Part 3), 369-390.

Davies, M., Rhode, M., Green, V. Clinical commentary XIV. *Br. J. Psychother.*, 1993, 9(4), 476-488.

de Ulhôa, C.E.M. Notas à margem de pensamento de Bion. [Notes in the margin of Bion's thought.] *Percuso: Revista de Psicanálise*, 1989, 1(2)[1], 10-17.

[Port.]

de Ulhôa, C.E.M. Thalassa: Matriz de hipóteses kleinianas. [Thalassa: Matrix of Kleinian hypotheses.] *Percuso: Revista de Psicanálise*, 1993, 6(10)[1], 56-63. [Port.]

Dervin, D. "Them'd" to death: Kleinian psychodynamics and the politics of projective identification in the 1992 election. *J. Psychohist.*, 1993, 21(1), 115-131.

Eigen, M. Psychic deadness: Freud. *Contemp. Psychoanal.*, 1995, 31(2), 277-299.

Eskelin, T. La simbolització de la relació terapèutica. [Symbolization of the therapeutic relationship.] *Revista Catalana de Psicoanálisis*, 1992, 9(1-2), 15-29. [Catn.]

Etchegoyen, R.H. Psychoanalytic technique today: A personal view. *J. Clin. Psychoanal.*, 1993, 2(4), 529-540.

Etchegoyen, R.H. Psychoanalysis today and tomorrow. *Int. J. Psycho-Anal.*, 1993, 74(6), 1109-1115.

Feldman, E. & de Paola, H. An investigation into the psychoanalytic concept of envy. *Int. J. Psycho-Anal.*, 1994, 75(2), 217-234.

Feldman, M. Projective identification in phantasy and enactment. *Psychoanal. Inq.*, 1994, 14(3), 423-440.

Ferro, A. From halucination to dream: From evacuation to the tolerability of pain in the analysis of a preadolescent. *Psychoanal. Rev.*, 1993, 80(3), 389-404.

Fink, K. Symmetry: Matte-Blanco's theory and Borges's fiction. *Int. J. Psycho-Anal.*, 1994, 75(5-6), 1273.

Fink, K. Matte Blanco Symmetrie und Bi-Logik. [Matte-Blanco's symmetry and bi-logic.] *Zeitschrift für Psychoanalytische Theorie und Praxis*, 1994, 9(4), 427-438. [Germ.]

Fink, K. Projection, identification, and bi-logic. *Psychoanal. Q.*, 1995, 64(1), 136-152.

Gadt, J.C. The "new" democratic woman of modernity: Georgia O'Keeffe and Melanie Klein. *Amer. J. Psychoanal.*, 1994, 54(2), 173-184.

Gilch-Geberzahn, G. Projektive Identifikation um psychoanalytischen Prozess [Projective identification in the analytic process.] *Forum der Psychoanalyse: Zeitschrift für klinische Theorie & Praxis*. 1994, 10(3), 260-273. [Germ.]

Grotstein, J.S. Projective identification and countertransference: A brief commentary on their relationship. *Contemp. Psychoanal.*, 1994, 30(3), 578-592.

Grotstein, J.S. Projective identification reappraised. *Contemp. Psychoanal.*, 1994, 30(4), 708-746.

Grotstein, J.S. Orphans of the "Real": I. Some modern and post-modern perspectives on the neurobiological and psychosocial dimensions of psychosis and primitive mental disorders. *Bul. Men. Clinic*, 1995, 59, 287-311.

Grotstein, J.S. Orphans of the "Real": II. The future of object relations theory in the treatment of psychoses and other primitive mental disorders. *Bul. Men. Clinic*, 1995, 59, 312-332.

Hartkamp, N. & Esch, A. Projektive Identifizierung in der psychoanalytische Schlussbildung. [Prokective identification and psychoanalytic inference.] *Forum der Psychoanalyse: Zeitschrift für klinische Theorie & Praxis*, 1993, 9(3), 214-233.

Hayman, A. Some rematks about the "Controversial Discussions". *Int. J. Psycho-Anal.*, 1994, 75(2), 343-358.

Hill, J. Am I a Kleinian? Is anyone? *Br. J. Psychother.*, 1993, 9(4), 463-475.

Joseph, B. Ein Faktor, der psychischer Veränderung entgegenwirkt: keine Resonantz. [A factor militating against psychic change: Non-resonance.] *Psyche: Zeitschrift für Psychoanalyse und ihre Anwendungen*, 1993, 47(11), 997-1012.

Kavaler-Adler, S. The conflict and process theory of Melanie Klein. *Amer. J. Psychoanal.*, 1993, 53(3), 187-204.

King, P. The evolution of controversial issues. *Int. J. Psycho-Anal.*, 1994, 75(2), 335-342.

Lebovici, S., Kestemberg, E. The breast and breasts. *J. Child Psychother.*, 1993, 19(1), 5-28.

Lewis, M. A neo-Piagetian interpretation of Melanie Klein's theory of infancy. *Psychoanal. Contem. Thought*, 1993, 16(4), 519-559.

Likierman, M., "He drew my attention to my great gift for understanding children...": Some thoughts on Sandor Ferenczi and his influence on Melanie Klein. *Br. J. Psychother.*, 1993, 9(4), 444-455.

Meltzer, D. O conflicto estético: o seu lugar no processo de desenvolviment. [The aesthetic conflict: Its place in the developmental process.] *Revista Portuguesa de Psicanálise*, 1990, 8, 5-29. [Port.]

Meltzer, D. A propos d'un system d'atelier. [A system of workshops.] *Psychanalystes*, 1993, 48, 99-102. [Fren.]

Mitchell, S. A. Interaction in the Kleinian and interpersonal traditions. *Contemp. Psychoanal.*, 1995, 31(1), 65-91.

Mitrani, J.L. On adhesive pseudo-object relations: I. Theory. *Contemp. Psychoanal.*, 1994, 30(2), 348-366.

Moses, I. Projective identification and countertransference. *Contemp. Psychoanal.*, 1994, 30(3), 575-578.

Muniz de Rezende, A. Bion formador de analistas. [Bion, educator of analysts.] *Percuso: Revista de Psicanálise*, 1994, 7(2)[1], 27-32. [Port.]

Nigel, T. "The social worker as bad object": A response to Marguerite Valentine.

Br. J. Soc. Work, 1994, 24(6), 749-754.

Priel, B. Symmetry: Matte-Blanco's theory and Borges's fiction. *Int. J. Psycho-Anal.*, 1994, 75(4), 815-823.

Priel, B. The dialectics of aesthetic experience: An object relations perspective on narrative ambiguity. *Psychoanal. Contemp. Thought*, 1994, 17(4), 547-562.

Quinodoz, D. Interpretations in projection. *Int. J. Psycho-Anal.*, 1994, 75(4), 755-761.

Rabih, M. Microduelo, ansiedad de separación y dolor mental. [Micro-mourning, separation anxiety and psychic pain.] *Revista de Psicoanálisis*, 1993, 50(4-5), 999-1012. [Span.]

Raguse, H. Der Todestrieb als Streitpunkt in den Controversial Discussions in London 1941-1945. [The death drive as a matter of dispute in the "Controversial Discussions" in London 1941-1945.] *Zeitschrift für Psychoanalytische Theorie & Praxis*, 1994, 9(4), 385-404. [Germ.]

Rhode, M. Links between Henri Rey's thinking and psychoanalytic work with autistic children. *Psychoanal. Psychother.*, 1995, 9(2), 149-155.

Richards, A.K. Perverse transference and psychoanalytic technique: An introduction to the work of Horacio Etchegoyen. *J. Clin. Psychoanal.*, 1993, 2(4), 463-480.

Rodrigué, E. O analista das 100.000 hors [The analyst of the 100,000 hours.] *Percuso: Revista de Psicanálise*, 1994, 7(12[1], 5-11. [Port.]

Rosen, D.L. Projective identification and bulimia. *Psychoanal. Psychol.*, 1993, 10(2), 261-273.

Sandell, R. Envy and admiration. *Int. J. Psycho-Anal.*, 1993, 74(6), 1213-1221.

Schafer, R. The contemporary kleinians of London. *Psychoanal. Q.*, 1994, 63(3), 409-432.

Schafer, R. One perspective on the Freud-Klein controversies 1941-45. *Int. J. Psycho-Anal.*, 1994, 75(2), 359-365.

Schoenhals, H. Kleinian supervision in Germany: A clinical example. *Psychoanal. Inq.*, 1994, 14(3), 451-461.

Segal, H. Notes sobre la formació de simbols. [Notes on the formation of symbols.] *Revista Catalana de Psicoanálisis*, 1992, 9(1-2), 89-98. [Catn.]

Segal, H. Phantasy and reality. *Intern. J. Psycho-Anal.*, 1994, 75(2), 395-401.

Segal, H. Salman Rushdie and the sea of stories: A not-so-simple fable about creativity. *Int. J. Psycho-Anal.*, 1994, 75(3), 611-618.

Skelton, R.M. Bion's use of modern logic. *Int. J. Psycho-Anal.*, 1995, 76(2), 389-397.

Smith, T.E. Measurement of object relations: A review. *J. Psychother. Pract. Res.*, 1993, 2(1), 19-37.

Spillius, E.B. Varieties of envious experience. *Int. J. Psycho-Anal.*, 1993, 74(6), 1199-1212.

Spillius, E.B. Developments in Kleinian thought: Overview and personal view. *Psychoanal. Inq.*, 1994, 14(3), 324-364.

Spillius, E.B. On formulating clinical facts to a patient. *Int. J. Psycho-Anal.*, 1994, 75(5-6), 1121-1132.

Steiner, J. A tribute to Henri Rey. *Psychoanal. Psychother.*, 1995, 9(2), 145-148.

Steiner, R. Les controverses Anna Freud-Melanie Klein 1941-1945. Notes éparses sur l'exprit de temps, l'esprit de lieu et leur importance dans l'arrière-plan culturel des controverses 1941-1945. [Conference on the Freud-Klein controversies: Some scattered notes on the Zeitgeist and the Ortgeist, and their relevance in the cultural background of the "Controversial Discussions" 1941-1945. *Psychanalystes*, 1993-1994, 48, 63-96. [Fren.]

Tustin, F. Un error psicoanalítico común acerca de la repetición regresiva en los trastornos autistas en la infancia. [A common psychoanalytic error about regressive repetition in autistic disorders in children.] *Revista de Psicoanálisis*, 1993, 2, 203-219. [Port.]

Valentine, M. The social worker as "bad object". *Br. J. Soc. Work*, 1994, 24(1), 71-86.

Van Buren, J. Mother-infant semiotics: Intuition and the development of human subjectivity–Klein/Lacan: Fantasy and meaning. *J. Amer. Acad. Psychoanal.*, 1993, 21(4), 567-580.

Warshaw, S.C. Whatever happened to Kleinian child analysis? *Psychoanal. Psychol.*, 1994, 11(3), 401-406.

Webb, R.E. & Sells, M.A. Lacan and Bion: Psychoanalysis and the mystical language of "unsaying". *Theory Psychol.*, 1995, 5(2), 195-215.

Weisberg, I. The converging influences od Sigmund Freud, Melanie Klein and the *Bhagavad-Gita*: W.R. Bion, *Int. J. Com. Psychoanal. Psychother.*, 1994, 9(1), 19-23.

Weisberg, I. Linking theory to practice: Melanie Klein and the relational revolution. *Int. J. Com. Psychoanal. Psychother.*, 1994, 9(1), 77-84.

Williams, A.H. Notes on the interaction between prison staff and prisoners. *Free Assn.*, 1994, 4(32, Pt. 4), 519-526.

Yorke, C. Freud or Klein: Conflict or compromise. *Int. J. Psycho-Anal.*, 1994, 75(2), 375-385.

THE SFR TRANSLATION AND PUBLICATION FUND, INC.

was established in 1991, as a not-for-profit scientific organization. Its purpose is the publication of original psychoanalytic (but not limited to) works from and in previously neglected thematic and geographic areas.

All contributions are tax-exempt, Certificate no. 16-1406324. Contributions, proposals and inquiries may be sent to:

> The SFR Transl. & Publn. Fund, Inc.
> Attn. Executive Director
> 1 Marine Midland Plaza
> Binghamton, New York 13901
> USA

* * *

A Warm Welcome to

Journal of European Psychoanalysis
Humanities, Philosophy, Psychotherapies

For subscription information:
Telos Press Ltd., 431 East 12th St., New York, NY 10009

INDEX OF CONTENTS:
MELANIE KLEIN AND OBJECT RELATIONS, VOLUME 14

INDEX OF CONTENTS
MELANIE KLEIN AND OBJECT RELATIONS, VOLS. 1-14

The Journal of the Melanie Klein Society was founded in 1983. Beginning with 1989, volume 7, no. 1, its title was changed to *Melanie Klein and Object Relations*.

Index compiled by Florin V. Vladescu

SEND US THEIR ADDRESSES AND WE WILL SEND THEM INFORMATION ABOUT THE JOURNAL.
THEY WILL APPRECIATE IT AND SO WILL WE.

Please send information about the journal and subscription rates to:

(PLEASE PRINT)
Name_____

Address_____

_____

_____

Name_____

Address_____

_____

_____

Name_____

Address_____

_____

_____

Name_____

Address_____

_____

_____

esf publishers, 1996

WOULD YOU LIKE TO HELP YOUR COLLEAGUES GET ACQUAINTED WITH THE JOURNAL?

SEE OVER ▶

– PLEASE FOLD, TAPE ENDS TOGETHER AND MAIL – – – – – – – – – – – – – – – – – – –

Affix
postage
here

BUSINESS REPLY MAIL

esf publishers
Attn: Journal of M. Klein & Object Relations
1 Marine Midland Plaza
East Tower • Fourth Floor
Binghamton, New York 13901-3216
USA

‖ɪɪ‖‖ɪɪ‖‖ɪ‖ɪ‖ɪ‖ɪɪ‖‖ɪɪɪɪ‖‖ɪ‖‖ɪɪɪ‖ɪɪɪ‖‖ɪ‖‖ɪɪ‖ɪɪ‖ɪ‖‖

LIBRARY RECOMMENDATION FORM

To recommend this journal to the appropriate subject specialist in your library, please complete the form below and drop it off with your librarian.

I recommend that the library subscribe to the following journal:

JOURNAL OF MELANIE KLEIN AND OBJECT RELATIONS
Volume 15, 1997

On a scale of 1 to 5 (1=lowest and 5=highest) I would evaluate the importance and relevance of this journal for teaching, training and research purposes as: _____
(RANK)

RECOMMENDED BY

Name/Title_____

Department/School_____

College/University/Institution_____

Signature_____

SEND SAMPLE COPY TO:

Librarian_____

Library_____

College/University/Institution_____

Address_____

_____

_____

Telephone Number_____

esf publishers, 1996

LIBRARY RECOMMENDATION FORM

SEE OVER ▶

PLEASE FOLD, TAPE ENDS TOGETHER AND MAIL

Affix
postage
here

BUSINESS REPLY MAIL

esf publishers
Attn: Journal of M. Klein & Object Relations
1 Marine Midland Plaza
East Tower • Fourth Floor
Binghamton, New York 13901-3216
USA

IᴵᵢᵢᴵᴵᵢᵢᴵᵢᴵᵢᴵᵢᴵᴵᵢᵢᵢᵢᴵᴵᵢᴵᴵᵢᵢᵢᴵᵢᴵᵢᵢᴵᴵᵢᴵᴵᵢᵢᴵᵢᴵI